Praises for Pursued by Grace

"In Pursued by Grace, Colin offers an honest and candid perspective on the pain and difficulties that arise from a moral failure. He also describes the journey of hope and healing that is available for those willing to pursue restoration. He underscores the importance of the old adage, an ounce of prevention is worth a pound of cure, and this is so true in terms of ministerial health and wholeness."

**Rev. Craig Burton, District Superintendent
Eastern Ontario and Nunavut
The Pentecostal Assemblies of Canada**

"Truth, indeed, sets us free; not only the truth of who Jesus is, but also the truth of who we are. My friend, Colin Gittens courageously shares his story to encourage the reader to know their story. This book is Biblical, personal, practical and transformational. I am a firm believer that if you don't process your issues, your issues will process you. Colin courageously shares his story to encourage others to face themselves."

**Rev. Mark Hazzard
Missions Regional Director, Latin America/Caribbean
The Pentecostal Assemblies of Canada**

"Becoming their pastor, then friend I had the incredible privilege of witnessing God's grace on display in Colin and Dorselie's lives first hand. This book, and their lives are a powerful reminder of discovering God's very best even when we feel we are at our very worst. *Pursued by Grace* is an honest, transparent journey that is packed with wonderful redemptive and pre-emptive truths. Read this book and allow God's grace to catch you!"

Dr. J.D. Mallory
Lead Pastor, Gulf Coast Church
North Port, FL

"Colin writes with absolute candor. His journey will absolutely speak to many. Thankfully, God's grace is abundant."

Rev. Frank Patrick
Church Consultant

"*Pursued by Grace* is shockingly and refreshingly sincere. It was written from a place of absolute trust in and surrender to God. This book has the power to break the cycle of sin in the lives of readers, while simultaneously teaching them how to completely let go and fall into God's arms of grace especially in life's most difficult moments."

Sam Tita
Author of Radical Prayers Radical Results

His grace abounds!

Pursued by Grace

A Pastor's Restorative Journey

by
Colin A. Gittens

Foreword by Donald A. Lichi, PhD

FriesenPress

Suite 300 - 990 Fort St
Victoria, BC, V8V 3K2
Canada

www.friesenpress.com

Copyright © 2020 by Colin A. Gittens
First Edition — 2020

All rights reserved.

ISBN
978-1-5255-6334-8 (Hardcover)
978-1-5255-6335-5 (Paperback)
978-1-5255-6336-2 (eBook)

1. BIOGRAPHY & AUTOBIOGRAPHY, RELIGIOUS

Distributed to the trade by The Ingram Book Company

Contents

FOREWORD

"THERE IS NO seminary course I am aware of that deals with moral failure. The influence of one's background, a distorted self-concept, and brokenness, combined with pressures of ministry are all the stuff the enemy takes advantage of to bring disgrace to the Name of Christ, pain to the church, and brokenness to the offender and offended. And yet, mysteriously… amazingly, we are pursued by God's grace.

While I was privileged to be a small part of the healing process, I believe more importantly that this book stands as a testimony of the love of God and as a guide and teacher for prevention. The scriptural admonition is so true: "If you think you are standing firm, be careful that you don't fall!" (1 Corinthians 10:12 NIV). In enough detail to be instructive, Rev. Colin Gittens shares his story—painful at times—of his rise, fall, and restoration not just to ministry but to life itself. You will also experience the painful impact of Colin's choices on the one he loves most: his beloved wife, Dorselie. Indeed, she is a woman "full of grace". Colin does not minimize, deny, or shun personal responsibility. Rather, he opens the reader to his past and openly walks us through the steps of failure and the impact of his sin on his marriage, family, and church. He then describes the hard road of recovery and restoration.

I pray you never have to experience what Colin has. Thankfully, Colin's painful journey did not end at the bottom. God is good; His grace is powerful and through His grace, the love and forgiveness of Dorselie, a supportive community, and hard work, we witness personal testimony that from what the enemy intended for evil, God continues to bring good. I highly commend this book to you in the spirit in which it is written: with humility, transparency, honesty, and godly warning. Grace prevails.

Donald A. Lichi, PhD Psychologist
Vice President of EMERGE Counseling Services,
Akron, Ohio
Co-author, *Broken Windows of the Soul*[1]

---

1   Fleagle, Arnold R. and Lichi, Donald A. *Broken Windows of the Soul: A Pastor and Christian Psychologist Discuss Sexual Sins and the Prescription to Heal Them* (Chicago: Moody Publishers, 2011).

INTRODUCTION

SEPTEMBER 25, 2016 was a dark day for me. I recall waking up that morning. My stomach was in knots, my heart was beating fast, and my mouth was dry. Even though I was strongly committed to making a public confession before my congregation, nonetheless, I questioned in my mind whether I was making the right decision. But each time, I was convinced that what I was about to do was in everyone's best interest and therefore needed to be done. I recalled the many occasions on which I had taught the parishioners to be open and transparent about sharing difficult issues in their lives. It was now my turn to live up to my own preaching. Despite this knowledge, the uneasy feeling would not depart from me. Multiple bursts of anxiety rocked my world all through the morning, indeed, all through the two weeks preceding this most dreadful day.

On that unforgettable Sunday morning, I put on a brave face and walked into the sanctuary, smiling as I did every Sunday. However, my smile was masking the terror that lay within me. As I looked around the sanctuary and saw all the parishioners happily worshipping away, oblivious of the shocking news that was about to be dropped on their laps, I was wrought with guilt and shame; guilt, for how I was about to disrupt their church lives, and shame, for I knew that their perception of me was about to change for the worse. I glanced at my watch for the umpteenth time. The time was drawing nigh for me to get behind the pulpit, face the flock that I had pastored and ministered to for the past 22 years, and make a humiliating confession: A confession that their pastor whom they had grown to love and respect had failed them and broken their trust; a confession that I had committed the sin of adultery.

The above is just a preamble of what I will share in this book. What I found while writing this book is that it is quite a challenge to come up with original and captivating thoughts that have not already been shared by authors far more talented than I am. And thus, for this reason and others, I decided to place the emphasis of this work on a personal testimony of God's mercy and grace lavished upon me, as opposed to penning a "typical" book. The contents address the experience of a pastor who once experienced the awesome saving grace of God then regrettably fell into sin. But even in that failure, he was met with the unconditional and unmerited favour of his Lord and Saviour. I have learned that God in His providence will take what the enemy intended for evil and bring about good. But this good comes not as a result of sin, but in spite of it.

This is not the type of work that makes me feel I have accomplished something significant. No. It is not the type of testimony I am excited about sharing. On the contrary, once my story is told, I would prefer to move on to continue fulfilling the original purpose for which I was called into ministry. My personal mission statement captures this life quest succinctly. It is: "To be a channel through which the Holy Spirit can flow in order to bring many to the saving knowledge of Jesus Christ and then to see them discipled."

My hope is that my testimony will help to keep many from falling headlong into the sin of adultery or any other area of debilitating sins. My prayer is that the gravity of my sin will so grip the hearts of my readers that they would run far from the works of the flesh. To this end, I offer to you what I call *Pursued by Grace*.

Why *Pursued by Grace*?

As you will see, the repercussions of my sin were dire, crippling, and embarrassing. They were horrendous and punitive. They left no area of my life untouched: spiritual, relational, social, and financial. The losses in each sphere were debilitating and highly chastising. So why would I ascribe the word "grace" to such outcomes? After all, isn't grace defined as the unmerited *favour* of God? This being true, what then can be considered so favourable about such an oppressive journey?

To adequately address this seeming "paradox", one has to look at life from a different perspective, from a godly perspective, from an eternal perspective. First, we need to remind ourselves of these truths: "For God so loved the world that He gave His only begotten Son so that whoever believes in Him will not perish but have everlasting life." (John 3:16 NIV). "He who did not spare his own Son but gave Him up for us all, how will He not also with Him, graciously give us all things?" (Romans 8:32 NIV). These two verses are only a small sampling of Scriptures that demonstrate the depth of God's love for us and the high priority He places on saving us and setting us apart for the inheritance of His kingdom. No sacrifice is too great for Him to make for us. This is the God who leaves the 99 sheep in pursuit of the one that is lost. God is more interested in having us not gamble with our eternity than He is with our comforts, our positions, and our treasures. Both His rod and staff bring us comfort.

So yes, to the naked eye, the fallout of my experience looks like anything *but* loving, merciful, or gracious. But on the contrary, it has *everything* to do with God's love, mercy, and grace. God, being a loving Father, saw that his son had made a wrong turn on his life's path. And God sent His loving grace to pursue me, stop me in my tracks, turn me around, and bring me back into His fold.

For this I am truly grateful to Him. This kind of "reckless" pursuit of love can only be ascribed to my Almighty, forgiving, and faithful God.

Why Write?

I write because, as pastors, we rarely get the opportunity to tell our life-changing story. Over the years, hundreds of people have come to know me as Pastor Colin. In the public educational field, others know me as Mr. Gittens. But very few people know Colin. My hope, therefore, is that telling my story will communicate at least a few things:

- Pastors, like everyone else, are first of all flawed human beings.

- The main difference in the calling God placed on my life and the one He has placed on your life is simply a matter of time commitment. But we are all called to make an impact on the kingdom of God.

- While parishioners tend to hold pastors in high esteem, we also wrestle with the same challenges you experience. None of us are exempt from trials and temptations.

- Regardless of the pitfalls we may experience, God ultimately uses them all to bring glory and honour to His name.

- What is most important about our achievements in life is that we deeply love God and have a deep desire to transmit that love to others.

- Along with your gracious forgiveness of me, my hope is that the people I have betrayed will, in time, be restored.

I write because I want to share about a pastor's journey back to wholeness after having experienced a moral failure. In so doing, I hope that my temporary removal from public ministry will serve as a wake-up call to those of us who may be tempted to take for granted the privilege of being called to this sacred office. As has been aptly noted by one of my favourite authors, "The constant flow of failures among Christian leaders today in every denomination threatens the fabric of the church of Jesus Christ. Our credibility is being eroded among the people we have been called to reach because scores of failures among Christian leaders have created a cynicism toward the church within our culture."[1]

When we hear of moral failures involving sexual misconduct among prominent leaders, certain preconceived notions and stereotypes immediately come to mind. I, for one, think of and sympathize with the young/rookie pastor who is fascinated by the trust that comes with the office. As a result of his immaturity, he becomes a victim of the sin of adultery. I think of a pastor in his twenties or thirties, who has long entertained the enemy's temptations and has now gotten to a point where he may no longer be able to deal appropriately with the compliments, admiration, and sexual advances of those of the opposite sex. Inevitably and inexcusably, he ends up crossing the line and falling into sin.

While one may be prone to sympathize with a rookie/young inexperienced pastor, the sentiment changes drastically when the fallen pastor is older and more mature. To experience a moral failure as a matured leader is a totally different atrocity! It is downright ridiculous, shocking, embarrassing, inexcusable, and ultimately demonstrates a lack of discipline, among other virtues. This reckless behaviour of a seasoned pastor almost justifies the parishioners' loss of respect for and trust in him. It is an indiscreet act that seriously calls into question the pastor's moral compass. In short, this is bad! As we say among family members: "This is the giddy limit!"

The only thing more embarrassing than this is the fact that I have just accurately described myself! Nonetheless, I am aware that what causes us to struggle with sin is the fact that we have not yet fully discovered the dark depths and intricacies of our own hearts. My prayer is, therefore, that leaders in any stage of their life or ministry will be cognizant of the schemes of the enemy. Sin has never been a respecter of the position a person holds or their level of maturity, hence the reason why in one unguarded moment, it is possible to tarnish the achievements of a lifetime.

When my sin first became breaking news, as can be expected, people's reactions were varied. Some had negative feeling towards the news, while others gossiped. As I reflect on this, I cannot blame them for feeling this way. On the flip side, yet others responded graciously and lovingly. In extending their forgiveness to me, most of them uttered a statement similar to this: "Pastor, the love and grace you are receiving from us is exactly what you gave to us." If this sentiment is accurate, then

I ascribe all glory and honour to God for giving me the ability to have gracious and loving relationships with my congregants.

Like most fallen pastors, I never envisioned myself experiencing this sin, let alone writing about it. But it is also interesting to note that no one gets to choose which area of sin will plague them. Nonetheless, what may be worthy of recognition is this: I believe we are all born with a bent towards a particular area of sin. This does not mean, however, that we see this human weakness as a licence to sin.

Back in February 1984, when I felt the distinct call of God on my life to enter into full-time ministry, I had this conversation with God: "Father, I would be willing to abandon my teaching career to embark upon preaching, but God, if you know that I will bring grief and shame to your name, please *do not* place this responsibility on me!" So then, decades later, one might ask what happened to the answer of this prayer? In short, God certainly kept His end of the promise. I didn't.

Recently, I was reminded of this truth: "For we have this treasure in jars of clay to show that this all surpassing power is from God and not from us." (2 Corinthians 4:7 NIV). I recalled that God's treasure can never be contaminated by my sinful vessel. But more importantly, God, in His omniscience, knew that I was not going to keep my end of the bargain even before He called me into ministry—yet He called me anyway! This truth makes Him either the most gracious God ever or the highest risk taker!

After having one son, followed by three girls, my mom and dad prayed and asked God to give them another male child. This desperate longing of my mom was compounded with this promise she made: "Lord, if you give us another son, I will dedicate him to ministry." Months later, I arrived in this world.

Thanks, Mom. The first time this story was shared with me was on the day I revealed to my parents that I had felt a clear call from God to prepare for full-time ministry. I will never forget their response: "Son, that is not news to us. We knew that before you were born!" This gave me a fresh appreciation for Jeremiah's "dilemma": "Before I formed you in the womb I knew you, before you were born I set you apart; I appointed you as a prophet to the nations." (Jeremiah 1:5 NIV). I also observed that my mom had taken Hannah's predicament/vow seriously. "Lord Almighty, if you will only look on your servant's misery and remember me, and not forget your servant but give her a son, then I will give him to the Lord for all the days of his life." (1 Samuel 1:11a NIV).

I share this story with you to make this point: My calling was clear—both from the experience of my parents and from my own experience. God was faithful in answering my mom's prayer. However, I was disobedient in fleshing it out! But if my fall and removal from ministry can serve to help even one other leader from becoming prey to this sin, then telling my story would be worth it all. For some, this sin is committed mainly in thought and even sometimes in word. The more disciplined among us are able to avoid "crossing the line" by stopping short of sinning in deed. But nonetheless, we should remember Jesus' words: "You have heard that it was said, 'Do not commit adultery.' But I will tell you that anyone who looks at a woman lustfully has already committed adultery with her in his heart." (Matthew 5:27-28 NIV). This reality check clearly reveals how circumspect we need to be in this vulnerable area of life. It is a life-long challenge to us to live a consistently pure life in a highly permissive and sexually oriented society.

Because of the nature of this book, I do not feel it is appropriate to dedicate it to anyone. I am, nonetheless, majorly indebted to some close friends who have faithfully prayed for and encouraged me as I went through this horrific season of my life.

Three Godly Women

In my Christian leadership journey, I have encountered many prayer warriors and have experienced the positive results of their prayers. But three individuals stand out in my mind as women who have executed the ministry of prayer well. Eternity will reveal the powerful effect their prayers have had on my life.

The first person was a member of my home church in Windsor, Ontario. This saint, who is now with the Lord, had what I would call a direct channel or line to the throne room of God. One miraculous answer to prayer for my family stands out whenever I remember the ministry of this humble woman. But that story will have to be reserved for another time and occasion. Suffice to say, however, I always felt spiritually cared for whenever she prayed for me.

The second person was a servant of God I was introduced to in Jamaica, New York. I was a guest speaker at the church she attended. This was a growing congregation of more than 2,000 people. She was the first person I had ever known that was hired by her church just to pray! She came in to "work" every day at the scheduled time, went upstairs to a special prayer room that was set apart for this purpose, and prayed for eight hours! All the prayer requests from those attending that church were brought to her and she laid them bare before God. What a humble, gracious woman she was! What a ministry she was afforded!

The third person is a senior woman whose reputation for being an intercessor is well known in and out of her circle. Prayer has been her lifeline for decades. At her eightieth birthday celebration, folks from every generation took to the microphone and spoke about the impact her prayer life has had on them. These were awesome God moments that revealed a legacy that is second to none. Once I got to know her, or more accurately, once she got to know me, my name and ministry needs were added to her daily prayer list. One is indeed privileged to be known and loved by her. What a spirit she possesses! What a reputation to have! What powerful testimonies have been amassed from the answers to all her prayers!

I specifically recall the day I told her about my moral failure. I did so with fear and total embarrassment. I braced myself for what I anticipated was going to be a sharp rebuke, followed by an appropriate lecture about how shocked and disappointed she was to receive such news. But I will never forget the way she responded. She instantly went into prayer on my behalf. Her conversation with God included the claim that what Satan had intended for evil, God would turn around for good. She proceeded to bind any further schemes that the enemy might have planned for my life and prophesied that the next phase of my ministry was going to be much more powerful than the present. She concluded by comforting me with the thought that the love and respect she has for me would not change, and that I would always be her pastor. What grace! What a display of genuine Christian love! What a healing balm this was at a time when even some of my colleagues in ministry were understandably distancing themselves from me. God bless you, my dear sister. Whatever good comes out of this testimony, please be assured that some of it will be credited to the incredible Christian love you lavished on me that dreaded day of disclosure.

Why else do I write? I write because the Holy Spirit has impressed upon me that this form of transparency and vulnerability will, from here on, serve at least two purposes: 1.) It will remind me of how great my losses have been, including relationships, trust, finances, and effectiveness. 2.) It will, more importantly, hold me accountable for how I ought to conduct my moral life from this day forth.

My prayer, which complements the purpose for writing this testimony, is that my journey through this season of my life will accomplish at least two other things. First, that my downfall will graciously warn my fellow colleagues in ministry, leaders, small group facilitators, and every Christian person who picks up this book to not give Satan liberty in their life, especially in the weak areas. *Do not* be naive about his schemes and designs for your life. Rather, heed James' advice and flee the very appearance of evil and get rid of all moral filth. (James 1:21 NIV). Secondly, if you are presently dabbling in the sin of adultery, or any other sin for that matter, here is a word for you from the Lord: "Stop or be stopped!"

Acknowledgements

The mere fact that you are in possession of this book attests to the good work of a number of friends—some of whom are too humble to have their names shared. As is most often the case, this book has seen many drafts and critiques from friends, family, and colleagues alike. For their honesty and input, I am deeply grateful and would like to express my sincere thanks to them.

I would be remiss, however, if I did not express my gratitude to Dr. Donald A. Lichi. It has been accurately said that if you want to get a job done well, then ask a busy person to assist.

Dr. Don as we respectfully refer to him, was gracious enough to take a number of hours out of his busy work schedule to review my manuscript. My original request was for him to review and critique one chapter, but he took on the additional task of reviewing the entire manuscript and added several thoughts and suggestions that only can come from the vast experience he has had in the field of counselling. Dr. Don, my sincere thanks to you.

My district pastor, Rev. Craig Burton, has also been very instrumental in "fine-tuning" a part of this book. He spent valuable time clarifying a number of facts and shared values that we hold as a fellowship, especially in the area of restoration programs. I was blessed to have him walk with me throughout my entire restoration period and provide invaluable help to me, especially in the areas of counselling and accountability personnel. Thanks for caring, Craig.

Editing a manuscript is not an assignment for the faint of heart. You need friends and professionals to tell you the truth about what you have written and then correct the inaccuracies in love. I have been privileged to have such friends at my disposal—not just during this period, but throughout my life. You guys are the best! I am deeply grateful to you for your labour of love in editing, re-arranging, footnoting, and all the other work that was required to make this book possible. God bless you all richly.

Of course, at the top of this thank you list is my dear wife, Dorselie. I want to thank her for continuing to love me, putting up with me, and agreeing with me to publicly share my sordid story. As you might imagine, this was a very difficult season in her life. But God! Among the losses incurred by my reckless behaviour, I am most saddened by the fact that my removal from ministry also caused a disruption in the good leadership that Dorselie gave in many areas of the church. May God reopen this door for you, Dorselie, and make the next phase of your ministry much more effective than you could ever have imagined. All glory to God!

Chapter 1

MY FOUNDATIONAL YEARS

"Train a child in the way he should go,
and when he is old he will not turn from it."

Proverbs 22:6 NIV

EVERYONE HAS A life story. Have you ever told your story? If not, stop for a minute and ask yourself, "Why?" I suspect that there may be at least two reasons why we might hesitate to share our life's experiences. First of all, we may feel that our story is too boring, repugnant, or even morbid to tell. Secondly, we might have convinced ourselves that the negative incidences that had an impact on our lives date too far back in the past to matter. We rationalize that those incidences are now long behind us and therefore have very little or no relevance to the way we live our lives today.

Those two beliefs are not just untrue, but also sad. They are untrue because everything we have experienced, especially in the first fifteen formative years of our lives, is intricately related to who we have become as adults. Those beliefs are sad because if only we had the courage or insight to revisit our past through the knowledge and experience of a professional

1

counsellor, we would discover who we truly have grown up to be. They are also sad because for a major portion of our lives, we would have missed out on who God really wants us to be, and we would have been unable to connect the dots of our past with our present. Most unfortunate of all, they are sad because we would have lived most of our lives totally oblivious to some of the strongholds we have come to accept and believe as normal living. Whatever we choose to believe, the first fifteen years are our *foundation* years upon which we will consciously or subconsciously build our adult lives.

I speak from experience. Having grown up in what would be described as a good Christian home in which moral values were both taught and lived out, I disassociated any of my adult sinful behaviour from my childhood upbringing. After all, I had the benefit of enjoying several realities of which the average child living in North America today is deprived. Just to mention a few, I had:

- The privilege and stability of living in a two-parent home with six other siblings.

- The spiritual and biblical foundation of having family devotions five days a week.

- The blessing of having been taught the discipline of memorizing numerous passages of Scripture since I was about six years old.

- The model of a dad who loved his wife and children and more than adequately provided for all their needs.

- The benefit of having been taught gardening, carpentry, and several other trades since I was a child.

- The joy of attending worship services every Sunday as a family in the Moravian church.

- The exemplary Christian model of a mom and dad living out the faith in a practical manner.

- The blessing of not seeing my parents or siblings indulge in any vices such as gambling, swearing, spousal abuse, infidelity, alcohol consumption, etc.

If I were not speaking about the realities of life, one might entertain the thought that I lived in the perfect home. Not quite. I grew up in the 60s, in a third-world country, when the order-of-the-day belief claimed that to "spare the rod, (was to) spoil the child." This ancient proverb means: "If a parent refuses to discipline an unruly child, that child would grow accustomed to getting his own way."

Physical Discipline

In an under-developed country like Guyana, "good" parenting in the 50s, 60s, and even into the 70s meant that the following Proverbs were taken quite literally: "He who spares the rod hates his son, but he who loves him is careful to discipline him." (Proverbs 13:24 NIV). "Do not withhold discipline from a child; if you punish him with the rod, he will not die. Punish him with the rod and save his soul from death." (Proverbs 23:13-14 NIV). "Folly is bound up in the heart of a child, but the rod of discipline will drive it far from him." (Proverbs 22:15 NIV). Essentially, spanking was the "one-size-fits-all", foolproof method for disciplining a child for anything that was deemed wrong.

Unfortunately, this was also an age in which little emphasis was paid to the correct exegesis of Scripture. It was an era in which parents, teachers, and even extended family members believed that physical punishment was absolutely necessary to correct inappropriate behaviour and reinforce instruction. They believed that it averted long-term disaster, that children needed to physically feel the consequences of their sin and wrongdoing, and that failure to discipline in this manner would cause a child to grow up with an unclear understanding of what is right or wrong.

This faulty understanding of the Scriptures and the psychological fall out of the physical punishment I received revealed the following to me:

- Physical beatings did more harm than good, in that they stifled my academic development during my childhood.

- The word rod "indicates a thin stick or switch that can be used to give a small amount of physical pain with no lasting physical injury."[2] Or to put it another way, the child should never be bruised, injured, or cut by physical correction.

- Physical discipline was always intended to be done in love; never as a way of venting the frustration of the person administering it.

Regrettably, all of these lessons were violated. Consequently, beatings were administered excessively. Physical marks and welts were, on occasion, very visible on the bodies of children. Irreparable psychological, mental, and emotional damage characterized this period of our lives. Worst of all, academic growth and development in children was stunted; the very opposite of what the adults thought was being achieved.

I know this all too well. At the age of ten, I was a victim of classroom abuse. Mrs. Weaverpool, Mr. Owyn, and especially Mrs. Pain[3] were among the culprits (I really mean teachers) who contributed to the underdevelopment of my academic ability. Decades after having survived the clutches of these brutal educators, I was diagnosed by a professional counsellor as an "abused child"—a phrase I never would have associated with my upbringing. But in the 50s and 60s, I was regularly flogged for being an underachiever, both in primary and secondary school. It seemed as though that was the only way of "correcting" all problems that children faced growing up. If you were as "fortunate" as I was to have an aunt teaching at the school you attended, then you would recall receiving a double portion of beatings for your academic deficiencies. This was because when word of your beating got to your parents, they wanted to ensure you would never embarrass them again. Consequently, you received beatings part two! Looking back, it seemed to be a heartless period of our childhood life. Permit me to share one of the worst days of my primary school classroom experiences.

Mrs. Pain

It took me decades before realizing that this tyrant of a teacher lived out the meaning of her name in my life. Mrs. Pain caused me a lot of pain! In fairness to her, however, she probably felt that the disciplinary method of excessive flogging was indeed for the ultimate good of her students. Looking back at my experience in her Grade 6 classroom confirms to me that more than the physical pain she caused, she also inflicted a lot of physiological, mental, academic, and emotional damage to my life.

Five decades later, I still recall the day my spirit was broken in her classroom. The subject was Arithmetic. The problem was converting pence to shillings, and shillings to pounds, as British currency was used in our country, Guyana, in those days. On the day in question, Mrs. Pain stood over me with the intention of "helping me" to correctly carry pence to shillings and then shillings to pounds. I thought I understood how this was to be done, but probably required a little more time and patience to work out this sum. But as she stood over me with the wild cane in hand, I mentally froze and was unable to answer the questions she posed. As a result, I waited for and felt the first lash on my back. That was painful, but not as painful as the comments that accompanied it. In the hearing of the entire class, she charged me with being lazy and slothful in applying myself to my studies.

She compared me with my sister who was one of her star students. Then came the second lash, after which I was totally incapable of thinking mathematically. As she continued to ask the questions pertaining to solving the problem, all I could think about was when the third, fourth, and fifth lashes would descend on my back. Not a word came from my mouth. I sat at my desk and took the lashes and bore the pain and embarrassment that became my lot. As I heard some of my classmates snickering, I broke into tears. Death would have been most welcomed that day, but I was denied that out.

Things got worse for me that day. Mrs. Pain reported that classroom fiasco to my aunt, who also taught at that school. My aunt told me that my inability to perform simple mathematical equations was an embarrassment to her and demonstrated a lack of appreciation of the interest she took in my educational development. Because she lived a considerable distance from the school, she stayed at our house during the week and went home on weekends. This gave her the opportunity to share with my parents my underperformance that day and how belittled she felt.

Any West Indian person who lived in that era knows what followed next. That's right! Part two of the beatings was administered that night by my father. In addition, some sanctions were also set in place and additional homework was assigned.

Shutting Down

For the first time in my life, I felt psychologically abused. It started in the classroom and ended in our living room. I felt very angry at being academically misdiagnosed. I relived the pain of the lashes and the embarrassment I felt when my classmates snickered because they perceived me as dumb. I hated school. I wanted out. Unfortunately, I was not at liberty to express what I was feeling or experiencing with any adult. It would have been perceived as rudeness, insubordination, or ingratitude for all the sacrificial acts my aunt offered in order to provide me with a good education. Worst of all, any form of verbal response or retaliation would have ensured more beatings! So on such occasions, I would wisely shut down. Emotionally. Mentally. Academically. I learned quickly that I needed to protect my heart from further emotional abuse. So, like our suffering Saviour, (Isaiah 53:7 NIV) in my oppression and affliction, I felt like a lamb being led to the slaughter, so I chose to remain silent.

My purpose for re-examining my childhood is not to assign blame, but rather to gain a better self-understanding. And now, decades later, I have come to learn that this practice of suppressing my anger, which started at such a young age, was my way of protecting my heart.

McIntosh and Rima in their book *Overcoming the Dark Side of Leadership,* perfectly described my experience when they said: "Every leader has run the gauntlet of embarrassing and humiliating childhood experiences that have left their indelible mark." They go on to say, "These experiences are the very ones that must be explored and reflected on if we are to understand their full albeit subtle impact on our leadership."[4]

Discovering My Dark Side

McIntosh and Rima have a very interesting term they use to describe the way our personalities develop. They call it our dark side and explain it this way: "The dark side, though sounding quite sinister, is actually a natural result of human development. It is the inner urges, compulsions, and dysfunctions of our personality that often go unexamined or remain unknown to us until we experience an emotional explosion...or some other significant problem that causes us to search for a reason why."[5] This definition accurately describes what I discovered about myself during my restoration counselling.

The development of my dark side began with my experience in Mrs. Pain's class. The authors of *Overcoming the Dark Side of Leadership* add this revelation: "Without doubt, much of what determines how a leader's dark side develops, as well as how he or she will deal with the dark side once in leadership, stems from the family the person grew up in and his or her childhood years through adolescence. As we grow toward adulthood, our dark side begins to develop silently, only to emerge fully at some future date, often after leadership has been attained."[6]

As late as this discovery has been, I am nonetheless thankful that my dark side was identified. It answered many questions I had previously posed to myself for which I was unclear about the answers. I am, therefore, very grateful for the lessons I have learned about my dark side, for when this is not identified, or if it is ignored, "...it drives even successful leaders to make unwise, impulsive, unethical, or immoral choices."[7]

One other sobering thought I learned about our dark side is this: In reality, we can never really eradicate it. Even though we can subdue and overcome it for significant periods of time, it is always with us. This is why before we ever have the incentive to overcome it, we need to understand the sobering results of failing to do so. It is also good to know that we all have a dark side, and as such, this "...does not make us sick or bad, just normal."[8] On the contrary, "When we choose to live in ignorance of our dark side and resist all attempts to understand ourselves, our spiritual adversary is able to keep us in bondage through a continuous flow of lies and deception."[9]

Yes, the Scripture does command us to train up a child in the way he should go. It is a noble discipline and admonition, but also one that unfortunately was misunderstood and misinterpreted by many caregivers during my childhood. Just reflecting on the truth of this verse as rendered in the New Living Translation, makes the world of difference in the way we view this command. "Direct your children unto **the right path**, and when they are older, they will not leave it." (Proverbs 22:6 NLT, emphasis mine.) In the process of helping our children choose the correct path, we are, however, rightly acknowledging that the path an individual child takes may differ slightly from each other.

Training in 50s Style

Three generations ago, the facts that each child has his/her own unique path and one size does not fit all were not recognized or accommodated. Parents somehow felt that if their children were all exposed to the same disciplinary measures and training in the home, they should all turn out the same way. We now know this is totally untrue. Instead, parents need to uncover the individuality and special abilities that God has given to each child. By the same token, they should be able to identify the academic and social make-up of each child and respect his/her unique deficiencies and inabilities.

I am presently witnessing the positive impact that quality training is having on our four grandchildren. Their parents, I believe, are doing a credible job of raising them in an environment that takes into account their individual abilities and make-up. I marvel at how they have made each of their children a study, and consequently, they draw out the best from each of them. While they do not condone or excuse ill discipline, as observant parents, they highlight and compliment the natural gifts in each of their children. By talking to teachers, other parents, grandparents, and coaches, they have been able to better distinguish and develop the capabilities of each child.

Training our children to remain on **the right path** obviously does not necessarily mean that there is *one* set of values they must follow. Instead, in a manner uniquely tailored to each child, let us direct, guide, train, and ultimately release our children to become the adults that God intends them to be.

With the help of therapists, we now know that there are at least five love styles that can determine how we love as adults. These are dependent on a number of factors to which we were exposed as children. Milan and Kay Yerkovich in their book *How We Love* identify these love styles as avoider, pleaser, vacillator, controller, and victim. These "love imprints", as they call them, all grow out of "a childhood reaction to anxiety prompted by a lack of comfort, affection, and emotional connection."[10] In Chapter 7, we will take a closer look at these, and specifically my love imprint and the impact it had upon my life. But suffice it to say, our love imprints are styles that aid and/or impair how we love.

FOR REFLECTION AND INTROSPECTION

1. Have you ever told anyone your life story? If not, why not?

2. Can you recall any traumatic experiences you might have had as a child? Have you been able to make the connection with who you have become as an adult?

3. In training your children, have you been guilty of passing on negative deposits/habits that you received as a child? If so, how can you reverse this?

Chapter 2

WHEN SECRETS ARE REVEALED

"For there is nothing hidden that will not be
disclosed, and nothing concealed that will not
be known or brought out into the open."

Luke 8:17 NIV

AS YOU CAN imagine, writing a book from the perspective of
one who had a moral failure is not easy. It is not a lone person's
sin; there are other parties involved, both guilty and innocent.
As such, one has to balance the desire to be transparent with
the need to protect the privacy and dignity of the other parties
involved. To this end, it is not my intent to share any details
of what transpired. Rather, my motivation for writing is to
caution, encourage, and edify others to avoid or stop walking
down this devastating road.

One of the benefits of going through a restoration process is
the fact that one has the time to reflect on what brought them
to this point and determine what needs to be done to bring
them back into close fellowship with God.

In the past, I foolishly prided myself in knowing that I have not been tempted in other common areas of sin life such as drunkenness, pornography, off or online gambling, embezzlement, etc. But today, I thank God for forgiving me of priding myself in this Pharisaic way of thinking. I know better now. My revealed sin has both humbled and reminded me that while the aforementioned were never areas of temptation for me, Satan most certainly had another plan for this self-righteous pastor.

Of course, we know that temptations are no respecter of persons. This is when it is good to remind ourselves that temptation is not sin. However, we need to be cognizant of the fact that "temptation needs to be dealt with as early as possible when it is still an urge, thought, fantasy, or idea." In their book entitled *Broken Windows of the Soul*, Fleagle and Lichi remind us of this truth: "When ignored, temptation tends to intensify to the point that if we do not take the Spirit's way of escape, we will be led to begin acting out—with the inevitable consequences."[11]

Looking back, I now see how ignoring temptation, coupled with my caring personality and the strong desire to help hurting people, created a perfect backdrop for my downfall.

Ministry Before the Fall

The situation at the church where I pastored was as follows. Staff relationships were great. The stability and longevity of our pastoral team were realities that spoke volumes about our church. We worked well together. I had a great board that was very supportive and worked with me to ensure that the mission and vision of the church were being fulfilled. While tithes and offerings could have always been better, we never experienced the type of financial stress that causes major concerns. The lay leadership in the church was exemplary. In short, I was enjoying ministry and working with a staff of 14 employees and over 150 small group pastors. Our weekly attendance at church services rarely fell below an average of 800 worshippers. In short, my ministry life was good. As Dr. Don Lichi would say: "Nothing fails like success."

Reminiscing afresh about this scenario reminds me of a similar situation King David faced before he committed adultery and murder. A brief summation of where David stood in his kingship reveals to us that after restoring the nation to peace and great military power, his personal life became entangled in sins. Recall with me how David went from being a highly successful king to committing sins that had far-reaching effects on generations to come. Between chapters 11 and 15 of 1 Samuel, we see how David's life spiralled out of control.

David's life was good. His army was powerful and unrivalled. Consequently, "In the spring of the year when kings normally go out to war, David sent Joab and the Israelite army to fight the Ammonites." (2 Samuel 11:1 NLT). The Scripture goes on to say that: "They destroyed the Ammonite army and laid siege to the city of Rabbah. However, David stayed behind in Jerusalem." In other words, there was no need for him to go to war because he knew how good his army was. So David abandoned his purpose and shirked his responsibilities by staying home from war. This "free time" led him to focus on his own desires (11:2). When temptation came, he looked into it instead of turning away from it (11:3). This caused him to sin deliberately (11:4). Next, he tried to cover up his sin by deceiving others (11:6-15). He then committed murder to continue the cover-up (11:15,17). Eventually, David's sin was exposed (12:9) and punished (12:10-14).[12]

In my case, the disconnect came as a result of putting ministry on autopilot. It is embarrassing to admit this, but I discovered in my ministry that when things were going well, at least two major temptations assailed me: 1.) My daily dependence on prayer and the Word were no longer crucial, and my prayer life became another ministry activity that I engaged in. 2.) I carefully chose to preach on topics that were safe and did not bring conviction to my life. At this point in my ministry, it dawned on me how large a percentage of ministry can be staged. This was very scary because while God was still working His purpose out in the lives of His people, His Holy Spirit had already bypassed me. Just as appalling, I found I was deceiving myself into believing that I was not that sinful after all, since many congregants were still being blessed and discipled.

Many may ask at this stage, "How is it that you were able to continue preaching when the person you were involved with was sitting in the congregation?" For me, I comforted myself by going through the motions of asking God to forgive me of my sin and to continue to use me to reach His people. This dynamic is called "brain reward" mechanism.

When this "prayer" appeared to be answered, and I saw God move in the church, I felt *temporarily* absolved of my guilt and justified to continue standing behind the pulpit. I use the word "temporarily" because the enemy of my soul would mock me in my quiet moments. He would remind me that: 1.) I had preached about the perils of this sin. 2.) I had been called to model and live at a higher standard as a Christian leader. 3.) My behaviour perfectly confirmed the accusations of those who saw us as being hypocritical.

Today when I see how much people struggle with sin of all kinds, and when I ponder my own personal struggles, I gain a fresh understanding of Apostle Paul's heart's cry: "And I know that nothing good lives in me, that is, in my sinful nature. I want to do what is right, but I can't. I want to do what is good, but I don't. I don't want to do what is wrong, but I do it anyway. But if I do what I don't want to do, I am not really the one doing wrong; it is sin living in me that does it.

"I have discovered this principle of life—that when I want to do what is right, I inevitably do what is wrong. I love God's law with all my heart. But there is another power within me that is at war with my mind. This power makes me a slave to the sin that is still within me. Oh, what a miserable person I am! Who will free me from this life that is dominated by sin and death?" (Romans 7:18-24 NLT).

Today, I am delighted to say that I have made the transition found in the first verse of Romans chapter 8 which says: "Therefore there is now no condemnation for those who are in Christ Jesus, ..." So, to answer Apostle Paul's question, who can free us from the power of sin? The Lord Jesus Christ through the power of His Holy Spirit! Glory to His wonderful name! We do not have to be hopeless and crippled by the power of sin.

Close friends of mine have asked: "Wasn't there at least one person that you could have confided in and shared your struggle with?" First of all, sin—especially sexual sin—has a devious way of thriving in an environment of secrecy. But the reality of the matter is this: If you can identify one such true friend in your life, you are very blessed. What I have observed over the years is that we really don't have caring friends that we trust implicitly. The person we consider our confidant inadvertently has another friend that they share with and confide in, who also has a friend that he/she confides in. You get the picture I'm sure. In short, confidentiality has become a foreign concept.

I have seen close and long-standing friends betray each other's trust without giving the situation a second thought. This has led me to believe that "confidentiality" has either lost its true meaning, or it has been redefined to fit the behaviour pattern of our culture. Consequently, we tend to hold back from sharing our true confessions in fear that our deep, dark secrets and sins will also be shared with others. We hold back full disclosure because we fear that the skeletons in our closet may be much scarier than the ones in the other person's. So, here is what we are prone to do instead. We "test the waters" by sharing just enough of the dark areas of our lives, with the hope that our confidant has the sensitivity or spirit of discernment to listen to what we are not saying and to offer us the help we need. If this does not happen, we are somewhat relieved because we protected ourselves from deeper hurts by not being too vulnerable. As a result, we rarely get past the surface or shallow levels of relationships, and we fail to disclose the sins and struggles we are experiencing.

What does all this mean from a pastoral or leadership perspective? First of all, I believe that many of us do not have someone in our lives with whom we can honestly share our deepest thoughts and challenges. We live in a social media culture in which we have many acquaintances but few real friends. I refer to the kind that sticks closer than a brother. We therefore tend to protect ourselves by holding back from being authentic and transparent Christians. Instead of getting to know us "by our love one for another", Christians and non-Christians alike get to know each other by our lack of transparency.

"My Sin, Not in Part but the Whole..."

During my period of restoration, I gained strength from the words of the hymn penned by the writer Horatio Spafford entitled, "It Is Well with My Soul". I was particularly touched by these words: "...my sin not in part but the whole is nailed to the cross, and I bear it no more, praise the Lord, praise the Lord, O my soul." That was also my experience. This is the only reason why I can now freely talk about my reckless, sinful behaviour. Thankfully, in God's eyes, I am forgiven and restored! For me, this is the first and most important part of restoration: the re-establishing of my intimate relationship with God. However, at first this was not easy to achieve.

During my time of restoration, as I had anticipated, I encountered every possible reaction to my sin. There were those who were deeply disappointed, and others who had a very difficult time coming to grips with my behaviour. And so I would like to take the opportunity here to specifically address my previous church family and Christian friends: From the depths of my heart, I am truly sorry for sinning against you. I am sorry for the negative impact this must have had on your relationship with God, and possibly with other pastors.

Secret Versus Open Confession

This question was asked by someone: "Pastor, how could you engage in an adulterous relationship and still preach the Word?" And the answer, to my shame, was this: By consoling myself with the fact that once I had asked God to forgive me, He had forgiven me. And while that might have been true, I became blind to the grief this was causing my Lord. I merely tried to ease my guilty conscience by telling God how sorry I was. That is the power of sin and secrecy. That is the problem with private confession! We are accountable to no one.

Andy Stanley, in *Enemies of the Heart*, articulates the problem with secret confession when he says: "We can be repeat offenders without embarrassing ourselves.... In fact, that's exactly why we confess secretly: In many cases we know we're going to repeat the offense." On the contrary, "Open confession has the power to break the cycle of sin."[13] Therefore, if we truly want to break this cycle of sin and guilt, we need to confess the way God designed confession to be applied and determine to live God's way. This is my plea and prayer for all of my readers who are aware of any sin that easily besets you. Like the fruit of sin, "Temptation comes in many forms, but it is always personal, uncannily tailor-made for our individual moral weakness, and it takes aim at God's character, seeking to ransack our faith."[14] If we can identify with this truth, then let's be honest and get the help we need.

Looking back at this period of my life, what I failed to recognize was the fact that my struggle was not just to overcome debilitating temptation and sin, but rather to realize I was in the midst of a spiritual battle. This wasn't just a "need to work harder at self-control" situation. Andy Stanley accurately articulates it this way: "Our battle for sexual purity must be waged on several fronts." He goes on to make this point: "Confessing, forgiving, celebrating, and giving are habits that strengthen our resolve and remove the enemy's base of operation in our lives."[15]

Lying

The sin of adultery, probably like other grave sins, has two first cousins: lying and deception. I sometimes refer to lying as a default universal sin. It kicks in whenever we face guilt and shame. We all succumb to this sin at some point in our lives, especially when we find ourselves in compromising situations and are fearful that the concealed truth will be revealed. Those who claim they do not lie, tell half truths. "A sin of commission occurs when you do something you know to be wrong. A sin of omission occurs when you let something bad happen when you could do something to stop it."[16]

In *12 Rules for Life*, Jordan B. Peterson addresses some of the ways in which we conduct our lives that make us prone to lying. We find ourselves crafting our speech and actions in a manner that would cause us to lie for one or some of the following reasons: to prove that I am right; to appear competent; to avoid responsibility; to be promoted; to attract the lion's share of attention; to ensure that everyone likes me; to garner the benefits of martyrdom; to justify my cynicism; to be politically correct; to rationalize my antisocial outlook; to minimize immediate conflict; to capitalize on my vulnerability; to always appear to be the sainted one; and so on.[17] These are what the Austrian psychologist Alfred Adler called "life-lies". I was reminded that when we betray ourselves and say untrue things, we weaken our character.[18]

Peterson continues: "And why not lie? Why not twist and distort things to obtain a small gain, or to smooth things over, or to keep the peace, or to avoid hurt feelings?"[19] As a child growing up in our family, I must confess, lying saved me from many a beating. As an adult, I must also admit that on the odd occasion, I found it was much less stressful to lie than to uphold the truth. And I'm probably not alone in this practice. I'm sure most of us can relate to Peterson's statement. But the Word reminds us that when we speak the truth in love, not only will we "...grow up into Him who is the Head, that is,

Christ," (Ephesians 4:15b NIV), but also we will be spiritually set free by the truth of the Word. (John 8:32 NIV).

Deception

Similar to lying, the sin of deception is what makes it very difficult for Christians who struggle to forgive their fellow brothers and sisters. Unfortunately, I know about this first hand. For the period I chose to conceal my sin, it made me look like a respected pastor whose life was "above reproach". I justified my ability to preach by ensuring that I had asked God to forgive me and to use me despite having grieved the Holy Spirit. Pastors beware! God is gracious enough to flow through a sinful vessel and touch the lives of those who have the faith to believe and receive what the Holy Spirit has in store for them. However, the problem is obvious to those of us who attempt this cover-up job: We mistakenly believe that what the Holy Spirit accomplished through our message was as a result of our studious preparation, prayer of confession, and delivery. We sometimes con ourselves into believing that asking God for forgiveness leads to Him affixing His stamp of approval upon our lives and ministry. Wrong! Were it not for the fact that God permits us to have "…this treasure in jars of clay, to show that the surpassing power belongs to God and not to us", we can accomplish nothing for Him. (2 Corinthians 4:7 ESV). At the end of the day, we would only be deceiving ourselves.

In the verse quoted above, in saying, "…we have this treasure in jars of clay to show that this all-surpassing power is from God and not from us," Apostle Paul reminds us why God can still flow through us. It is simply to show that this all-surpassing power is from Him, not from us. It is so comforting to know that my deformed jar of clay did not hinder the Holy

Spirit from accomplishing the work He wanted to do in the lives of His people. Or to put it another way, my imperfect jar of clay does not obstruct the work of the Holy Spirit. He has the power to work through even sinful vessels and accomplish His life-changing work. So while I was compartmentalizing my sin, God was being long-suffering with me. Friends, don't fall into this degenerate state in your life or ministry. This is deception at its worst!

What About My "Call"?

Several have either asked or pondered the following questions: What is it that caused you to compromise your "call" to ministry and succumb to this sin? At the end of the day was it worth the risk? Did you at any point seriously take into account how devastating this would be if you got caught? Did you factor in the immense loss you would suffer when this sin came to light? Did you consider the physical, relational, emotional, and financial ramifications? Was it *really* worth it?

In response to these questions, I may be tempted to give "the flesh" bad press—but not so fast! This is, in essence, a heart issue. Dallas Willard in *Renovation of the Heart* says, "… trained in a world of wrongness and evil, the body comes to act wrongly 'before we think' and has 'motions of sin in its members', which as Paul said, may thwart the true intent of our spirit or will by leaping ahead of it. 'It is not me…but sin that dwells in me!'" (Romans 7:17 PAR).[20]

Paul elaborates on this thought some more in Galatians 5:17 NLT: "The sinful nature wants to do evil, which is just the opposite of what the Spirit wants. And the Spirit gives us desires that are opposite to what the sinful nature desires. These two forces are constantly fighting each other, so you are not free to carry out your good intentions." Wow! I would have been quite relieved if this explanation could have been used as an excuse for my sin. I wish the answers to these questions were as easy as typing them. These are real and painful questions for any offender to honestly answer.

In Ray Carroll's book, *Fallen Pastor*, he shares about one Pastor Gary who had developed a meaningful relationship with Tina before his adulterous affair was brought to light. In retrospect, as he reflected on this truth, he said this: "The sin of adultery messes you up like no other sin. You become so connected to that person you feel responsible for them, and it's hard to break that connection. It becomes addictive."[21] Unfortunately, I can identify. And the best, most honest, well-crafted answers will still never suffice, let alone justify this repulsive act.

Nonetheless, the testimonies of numerous pastors who have fallen over the years, while different, reveal that the actual sexual encounter was just a small part of some bigger issues that were prevalent in their lives at the time. In other words, there are real origins, some subtle others blatant, that cause a pastor to go from a place of trust to a place of experiencing moral failure. Here is a very real struggle: When the pastor's need for someone with whom to share the stresses of life or ministry are not met, a real problem begins to brew. And worse, when that confidant is not his spouse, for justified or unjustified reasons, a substitute inevitably emerges. If the relationship with the "substitute" is not properly managed and confined within specific boundaries, an emotional connection develops and at that point, the possibility of crossing the line becomes less of a "what if" issue, but more of a "when" issue.

"D" Day!

"For there is nothing hidden that will not be disclosed, and nothing concealed that will not be known, or brought out into the open." (Luke 8:17 NIV). Every time I came across this verse in my devotionals or otherwise, it always sent a chill down my spine. I shuddered to think that the truth of this Scripture could one day be made manifest in my life. But I deluded myself into thinking that since the sin was behind me, and I had asked God to forgive and cleanse me, this particular verse did not necessarily have to be my portion. But alas! How wrong I was! True to this verse, my secret sin was discovered, exposed, and brought to light for all to see, and in a manner that I could never have envisioned!

As the Sunday approached for me to make a public confession before my congregation, I felt as if my world, indeed my life, was about to end! The first immediate fall out of my sin being exposed culminated in my loss of nine pounds in seven days. Sleep became a rare commodity, and the deprivation of dozens of hours of it began to show. I was forced to turn to medical help to arrest this situation.

During these horrible days, every thought, every precaution, every Holy Spirit warning that I had sensed prior to being busted, suddenly came flooding back to my mind with the express purpose of tormenting me. The reality that I had just lost the trust of my wife and the numerous lives I had touched in the past compounded the shame and the guilt I was already feeling. Fear and embarrassment became my closest companions. Every negative emotion you can feel rapidly gripped my heart. It was overwhelming. The realization of how grave this sin was began to sink in. The far-reaching consequences of my selfish behaviour and the fall out that would ensue scared me.

My first natural response was to leave town as quickly as possible for some quiet place to be alone.

However, through the counsel of a few key individuals in my life, I decided to muster up the strength and do the honourable thing to stay and make a public confession of my sin. The thought that I had ministered to this congregation for twenty-two years, coupled with the fact that we are a highly relational people, were two compelling reasons to face the music and fess up. But before I could make the public disclosure, I had to first break the news to my children, close relatives, and some very dear friends of ours whom we deeply love and respect. This had to be done in person. I was faced with the questions: Who really needs to know *before* I go public? And how much do I need to disclose? What about my dad and relatives back home? One of my siblings counselled me to spare my dad the pain and disappointment of this news. She feared what it might do to his health. But at the end of the day, I knew the need for confession was clear and I did it. When I drew up my "short" list of those I needed to tell first, it had 51 people! I knew that I would have a busy week ahead of me.

To put it mildly, confessing to each person was a painful, heart-wrenching exercise. I carefully monitored the shock that suddenly came over the face of each person as I moved from house to house to once again break the news. Like David, I was experiencing what he meant when he said, "For I recognize my rebellion, it haunts me day and night." (Psalm 51:3 NLT). I was forced to acknowledge the reality and devastation caused by my moral failure. Every time I shared my well-rehearsed lines with the next person on my disclosure list, the weight of my felony was deeper felt in my spirit. It was awful! Excruciatingly painful! The severe consequences of my sin were beginning to dawn on me. I had reached my breaking point.

I made a quick decision to prepare myself for the comments I anticipated I would hear from various congregants—retorts like: "I would have never thought my pastor would do something like that!" "I wonder how long this was going on?" "The pastor failed to live up to what he preached." "You mean to tell me that while you were doing this, you were still preaching?!" And on the more human and inquisitive side, "I wonder who the woman is?"

Real or imagined, these thoughts flooded my mind 24/7. Satan was having a heyday. He had caught a big fish! He was successful in bringing me to the place where I felt the full weight of shame and humiliation. Words cannot describe this season.

Carroll accurately captured the depth of shame I was experiencing when he said, "Shame is a form of internal judgment that devalues the inherent, God-given worth of the individual. It comes about when guilt turns into self-judgment, and the pastor reminds himself of former sin."[22]

All of the foregone found its climax on the Sunday morning of September 25, 2016, when it was time for my secret sin to be publicly confessed.

FOR REFLECTION AND INTROSPECTION

1. Why are sexual temptations so hard to resist yet the price is so high?

2. Is lying one of the sins you struggle with? If so, what causes you to lie, and what can be done to eradicate this sin from your life?

3. What sins have you not been honest with God about? Do you have a secret sin or unchristian-like behaviour that you need to confess? What is holding you back from confessing these sins to God?

Chapter 3
PUBLIC CONFESSION

"Confess your sins to each other and
pray for each other so that you may be healed."

James 5:16a NLT

ON SEPTEMBER 25, 2016, a little over two weeks after my sin was revealed, I stood before our congregation of over 700 people and made this confession.

"Dear PPC family,

My heart is broken today because I have let you down in the worst of ways. I am here to confess to you that I am guilty of a moral failure involving sexual misconduct. In the past, when my portfolio required a fair bit of counselling, I became involved with one of our parishioners and committed this grave sin against my wife, my family, and you my church family. And as a result, I have submitted my resignation as Pastoral Team Leader and my ministerial credentials with the Pentecostal Assemblies of Canada (PAOC) have been suspended. This is the last time that I will address you as your Pastor.

While I know that God has forgiven me, I am, nonetheless, painfully aware of the fact that sin has its consequences. I sinned against all of you—my church family—the very people that I promised to lead with integrity. I am ashamed—hence the reason why these words are the most difficult for me to utter.

PPC you are my friends. I love you dearly. You gave me the privilege of humbly serving you and making disciples among you, as you served God. It was the honour of my life. I stand before you a broken person, sorry and embarrassed, and taking full responsibility for my actions and asking that you find forgiveness in your hearts.

Going forward:

I have committed to go through a restorative program that our PAOC fellowship provides and have begun the healing process in my family. Beyond that, my future is uncertain. But my faith is strong— my unwavering faith in God and my belief in each of you. This knowledge, anchored deep in my heart, gives me a measure of solace—even through this failure in my ministry and most difficult phase of my life.

PPC, this is my prayer for you: that you would continue unwavering in your faith to love and serve God and make disciples. My singular hope; my solitary prayer is that you continue to seek God with all of your heart, all of your soul, and all of your mind. Your faith in God will never let you down. I have wronged you. He never will.

Over the last 22 years, I have received nothing but love and acceptance from you. I have experienced the joy of being able to serve with you. Thanks for granting me this privilege. Thank you for making my time here at PPC the most joyous days of my life. Thank you for welcoming my family into your hearts and into your homes. I will treasure these memories of you forever.

PPC you will constantly be in my prayers. I love you."[23]

This was one of the most difficult things I have ever done in life. At first when my sin was discovered, I had planned to have my confession read in my absence on that dreaded Sunday. However, as I reflected on what this would mean for me and for the congregation, and the message I would be sending, I knew that open confession was the right thing to do. I was also reminded of this truth: "How we respond when we have sinned reveals a great deal about the reality or unreality of our professions of faith."[24] I wholeheartedly concur.

The Congregational Response

What followed was a response I will never forget. The confession of my sin triggered an amazing outpouring of emotions from my parishioners. I found out, first hand, that true confession is a humbling experience. I had preached for many years about the seriousness of sin and how we ought to be God-fearing and honest in asking for forgiveness, but now it was my turn to live up to my own convictions. To say the least, this was a very vulnerable and sobering moment for me, but also very freeing.

Many cried out loud as the entire congregation spontaneously rose to their feet, adding applause to their standing ovation! Their reaction confused me at first. I had just blundered through the most horrific and embarrassing confession of sin, and our people applauded! Why? The reason for their applause became apparent to me as I observed scores of congregants lining up after both services to hug us and share in our grief and loss. I saw church family closeness displayed at its best. I overheard one person say, "This feels like being at a funeral." Many commended me for having the courage to take responsibility for my sin and to publicly ask for forgiveness. Others felt that I was forced into making a public confession. So even in that hour of grief, I felt compelled to take the time to correct their erroneous understanding.

Some of the testimonies shared that day included the following:

- Pastor, we understand things of this nature happen in life, but we still love you and respect you as our pastor.

- Pastor, you need to forgive me for taking your ministry for granted and for not praying for you as I should.

- Pastor, you taught me today how to own up to my sin and shortcomings. I will do this going forward.

- Pastor, I have always respected you, but today, by you mustering up the courage to publicly confess your moral failure, my respect for you has risen immensely.

- Pastor, this is the best "message" you have ever preached. When I consider the circumstances under which you made your confession, it encourages me to be more transparent and live my life with authenticity. Thank you for showing us this example.

- Pastor, unfortunately I too have experienced moral failure, but until now, I have never had the courage to share this with anyone! Thanks for being honest and transparent.

- Pastor, you haven't failed us; rather you have taught us how to honestly take responsibility for our sins.

Many more such "condolences" were shared with us that day, but there is one I will remember for a long time. The person who shared this testimony was visiting our church for the very first time. Being made aware of her presence, one of our leaders serving at our Information Desk wisely made an apology for the way the service had gone and for the confession I had made. The response of our visitor was something to this effect:

"In all of my church life I have never seen a pastor that stood before his congregation and honestly confessed his sin. The church I am coming from also went through the experience of our pastor having moral failure, but his response was totally different. He denied it ever happened, and consequently did not make a public confession and ultimately destroyed and split the church. Had he done what your pastor did, I would not have been here today. So I would like to make this church my new church home!" While I was truly saddened by this woman's experience of pastoral moral failures, I was also quite encouraged by the way she processed what I had shared that day. Even through this sinful confession, God somehow received glory. Amen!

While my public confession and the positive congregation's response helped me to get over the initial public disclosure hump, that was only the beginning of my healing. I was yet to traverse the long, arduous restoration journey that lay ahead of me.

On the inside, I was dazed by the fact that I would have to give up all aspects of ministry: the various boards I sat on, the leadership groups I was a part of, my position as lead pastor, the respect many had for me, etc. I was haunted by the fact that I had personally authored my own failures and losses by the selfish decisions I had made along the way. The reality that I had disappointed many people began to dawn on me. In short, the consequences of my sin were beginning to crash in on me, and there was no way out. But what I was reminded of that Sunday is succinctly stated by Wilson et al. in *Restoring the Fallen*: "People will always be hurt by honest revelations. The source of the hurt, however, is not in the telling, but in the sin itself. Not telling only compounds the hurt."[25] That is so true!

As I bring this chapter to a close, I need to do a brief fast forward of my life. It is now four years later. The passing of time does indeed make a difference. The hurts have been healed. I am restored to my Lord and Saviour. Most close relationships have been restored. The "time-out" from ministry has served me well. I have developed a whole new appreciation and a fresh perspective for ministry. For these and other graces, I give God all the glory.

FOR REFLECTION AND INTROSPECTION

1. Find someone you can trust and confess that sin you know has been blocking your prayer life and separating you from the sweet union you once had with God.

2. Do you have difficulty sharing your inner thoughts with a close loved one? Are you fearful that they may think less of you or distance themselves from you?

3. After the enemy has reminded you of your sin, keep short records and confess your wrongdoing quickly.

Chapter 4

#METOO AND THE CHURCH

"Now the overseer must be above reproach,
the husband of but one wife…"

1 Timothy 3:2a NIV

IT WAS SAID of the men of Issachar that they "…understood the times and knew what Israel should do."[26] In the context of the verse, the word "understand" represents two words in Hebrew. The first comes from *yada*, to know, and indicates personal experiential knowledge. It implies a deep understanding, a keen awareness, a discernment, or a competence. The second word, *binah*, which means insight and discernment, emphasizes these men's faculty of understanding. It was God who gave them wisdom and knowledge so they can discern the times and seasons they lived in. (Daniel 2:21 NIV).[27]

This type of understanding is crucially important to us as pastors and church leaders, especially in this media-driven age in which we live. Too often, the church has been criticized for lagging behind as change agents and responders to what is happening in our society. But in 2017 and 2018, with the advent of the #MeToo movement, the moral fibre of leaders in every area of work in our society has been put to the test. Consequently, much of the secret sins of men in high positions of power and authority have been brought to light, and in some cases, the consequences have been severe.

The #MeToo Movement

The #MeToo movement quickly became a stark reminder to us that we need to live lives that are above reproach in this permissive society. The statistics that appear below give us a glimpse into the impact this movement has had on all leaders. While most of the statistics shared are from the United States of America, they accurately reflect, on a smaller scale, what happens in Canada.

On the afternoon of October 15, 2017, actress Alyssa Milano tweeted the following: "If you've been sexually harassed or assaulted write 'me too' as a reply to this tweet."[28] Her tweet was in response to an October 5 *New York Times* investigation[29] into decades of allegations of sexual harassment against Hollywood Producer Harvey Weinstein. The "me too" hashtag went viral, garnering 14 million public tweets,[30] thus serving its intended purpose of bringing to light the magnitude of sexual harassment and assaults that women world over encounter.

It should be noted, however, that although Ms. Milano's tweet made the hashtag famous, the phrase "me too" was actually coined by Tarana Burke. According to Ms. Burke's website, "The 'me too' movement was founded in 2006 to help survivors of sexual violence, particularly Black women and girls, and other young women of colour from low-wealth communities, find pathways to healing. Our vision from the beginning was to address both the dearth in resources for survivors of sexual violence and to build a community of advocates, driven by survivors, who will be at the forefront of creating solutions to interrupt sexual violence in their communities."[31]

What followed, the #MeToo campaign, has been dubbed the "Weinstein Effect". Women world over began to break the shackles of silence, shame, and intimidation and candidly speak up for the first time about their experiences with sexual harassment and assault. As a result, many powerful, previously untouchable men were exposed and taken down by the #MeToo movement. It seemed like every day a new person was exposed and disgraced and fired (or resigned) from their powerful positions. I am sure this period was very nerve-racking for many who had skeletons in their closet, and I imagine it served as a wake-up call for all leaders who had been involved in or had entertained thoughts of sexual misconduct.

No one was immune: company executives, Hollywood personalities, politicians, media personalities, white-collar professionals, blue-collar professionals, even clergymen. According to an article by Bloomberg, as of October 5, 2018, one year after the Harvey Weinstein exposé, "At least 429 prominent people across industries have been publicly accused of sexual misconduct, a broad range of behaviour that spans from serial rape to lewd comments and abuse of power."[32] Bloomberg admits that its accounting is conservative, limited to publicly reported allegations, and excludes "instances of broader gender discrimination, non-sexual bullying, and racial insensitivity. A broader data set kept by crisis consultant Davia Temin puts the number of alleged bad actors at more than 800 people."[33] Per Bloomberg data, here is the breakdown of the people accused of sexual misconduct by industry:

- Government and Politics (96 people)
  - State and local government (63)
  - Federal government (21)
  - U.S. politics (6)
  - Judicial (3)
  - International government (3)
- Entertainment (96 people)
- Arts & Music (58 people)
- Other Industries (179 people)
  - Media (48)
  - Education and research (26)
  - Finance (25)
  - Consumer goods (23)
  - Other (15)
  - Sports (14)
  - Technology (7)
  - Medical (6)
  - Philanthropy (6)
  - Publishing (6)
  - Policy (3)

The #ChurchToo Movement

Hot on the heels of the #MeToo movement, the #ChurchToo Twitter hashtag was birthed in November 2017 by Emily Joy, in a bid to pull back the curtain and expose sexual misconduct in Christian circles. On May 31, 2018, *The Washington Post* published an article titled "The Sin of Silence: The epidemic of denial about sexual abuse in the evangelical church". The article highlighted how the evangelical churches fail to "report sexual abuse, respond appropriately to victims, and change the institutional cultures that enabled the abuse in the first place."[34] Offenders often go unreported because they repent of their sin, and as such, are considered forgiven. Victims are encouraged to show grace.

Churches struggle to maintain a balance between forgiveness and accountability and often choose to handle these cases internally using "biblical principles". As such, statistics on the occurrence of sexual misconduct in evangelical circles are not readily available. However, according to an article in *The New York Times*, "The three companies that insure a majority of Protestant churches say they typically receive upward of 260 reports a year of children younger than 18 being sexually abused by members of the clergy, church staff members, volunteers, or congregants."[35] Wade Mullen, the Director of the M.Div. program at Capital Seminary and Graduate School, conducted research as part of his PhD dissertation and found that in 2016 and 2017, there were "192 instances of a leader from an influential church or evangelical institution being publicly charged with sexual crimes involving a minor, including rape, molestation, battery, and child pornography." (This data did not include sexual crimes against an adult or crimes committed by someone other than a leader.)[36] Data from research done on 1,050 pastors in California in 2005 and 2006 showed that 315 (or 30%) of the pastors polled said they had either been in an ongoing affair or had a one-time sexual encounter with a parishioner.[37]

Yet another study[38] furnished these findings:

- 51% of pastors say that Internet pornography is a possible temptation for them.

- Approximately 20% of monthly calls to Focus on the Family's Pastoral Ministries Division are because of sexual misconduct and pornography.

- More than 30% of pastors are functionally addicted to Internet pornography.

- More than 15% of pastors engage in sexual behaviour that they consider inappropriate.

- 10 to 14% of pastors have sexual contact with someone other than their spouse while employed as a minister.

- There is an average of seven victims of clergy sexual misconduct per affected congregation.

This report on clergy isn't looking very good, is it? Viewed from a Christian leadership perspective, these statistics seem quite alarming. What could be fuelling these immoral behaviours?

We live in a society that uses sex to advertise and promote everything. Advertisers rely on the tried and true strategy of "sex sells" to guide their messaging and tailor their delivery. Pornography used to be something that was confined within the pages of magazines like *Playboy*. Not so today. We live in such a permissive society that we struggle to keep our thoughts pure while doing something as innocent as watching the evening news! We cannot even surf the Internet without being bombarded by pop-up images and advertisements with a sexual innuendo. These images that would be classified as "soft porn" have now been normalized and permeate all media with which we interact daily.

But what are some of the triggers that eventually end up ensnaring us? Here are a few:

- Subtle pressures of ministry demand that we find an out when stressed.

- Leadership takes a toll, leaving us with a great emptiness and a sense of no longer feeling the intimacy we once had with God.

- An incorrect belief that as God's representatives we can "fix" any problem or correct any wrong course of action in the lives of our parishioners.

- Great expectations placed on us that are hard to live up to.

- When ministerial stresses arise, there always seems to be someone of the opposite sex who is ready to be a listening ear.

- Compliments received from members of the opposite sex that come complete with an "open invitation" that seems to say, "*I am* available whenever you feel you need some help lowering your stress levels."

- A caring personality and a strong desire to help the hurting can draw a pastor into a co-dependent relationship with a broken-hearted parishioner, and if not managed well, it can form a perfect backdrop for the sin of adultery.

- A dark side that developed in us from our childhood that has been allowed to go unchecked for decades; consequently, we fail to associate it with our present sinful lifestyle.

Obviously, this list is far from being exhaustive, so feel free to honestly fill in your unique personal triggers. For those who are strong, disciplined, mature and do not have a bent towards sexual sins, I commend you. However, we all need to identify and be honest about the sin that easily besets us, and deal with it appropriately. Because this we know for sure: "… all have sinned and fall short of the glory of God." (Romans 3:23 NIV).

The Fallout of Sexual Misconduct Among Pastors

The recent stories and allegations of sexual misconduct of pastors, even world-renowned ones, have contributed to the erosion of trust and respect for the vocation. I personally apologize for contributing to this negative statistic.

Understandably, the majority of church members expect a minister and his/her family to live at a higher moral standard than themselves. Pastors are expected to live lives that are above reproach.[39] While this is not an unrealistic expectation from our parishioners, our failure to live up to this standard serves as a reminder that we too "have this treasure in jars of clay". Consequently, trust must ultimately be placed in God.

According to an article in *Desiring God*, when a pastor falls into moral failure, everyone is punished by his sin. "Reactions will range from confusion to disbelief to fury. Some will wonder how sin could capture the heart of someone God has used so powerfully in the church. Some will look for all the dirty details, secretly glad to see another gifted leader go down. Some will withdraw and rebel in disgust and anger, not willing to trust or submit to leadership in the church again."[40] What a sobering revelation! These reactions can unfortunately be expected because of the unrealistic pedestal upon which parishioners still tend to place their pastors.

Unfortunately, when one pastor falls, especially one that is highly revered and respected, it casts a shadow of doubt, scepticism, and mistrust over the entire vocation. Some parishioners struggle to understand why the pastor did not practice what he preached. Others wonder if they can trust any teaching from the pastor up to that point and are tempted to throw out any counsel or admonition ever received from him. Others may grow hopeless in their belief that they can overcome sin in their own lives, if the spiritual leaders who are supposed to be more mature, and should do better, succumb to temptation just as easily as they do. Perhaps the saddest consequence is that the weak Christians among them may see their very faith in God destroyed. All these consequences in turn negatively impact pastors' witness not only to their congregations, but also to unbelievers and society at large.

What Now?

I have just dumped a lot of depressing, but accurate information on your lap, haven't I? I would hate to close out this chapter on such a negative note. As such, permit me to share these words of encouragement to parishioners and leaders alike:

To the lay persons reading this, please understand that Christian leaders are human first, and clergy next. The same temptations that assail you are the same temptations that assail us—and I would go as far as to say, assail us even more so. The enemy knows that if he strikes the shepherd, the sheep will scatter and be easier to get to. And so I beseech you to not put your pastors on unrealistic pedestals. Do not put your faith in them but rather in Christ. And if they fail you, do not allow the enemy to plant seeds of doubt in your heart and mind. Do not let him tempt you to throw out your Christian faith on account of losing faith in Christian leadership. And finally, please do keep your leaders upheld in prayer. Sometimes requesting prayer in circumstances like these tends to seem so trite. But as one parishioner honestly shared with me the day I made my confession to the congregation, "Pastor, I take some responsibility for your situation as I have not prayed for you as often as I should have." As pastors, we are in a constant battlefield and covet your prayers of support and protection over us and our families.

To my fellow colleagues and leaders reading this, I know that the standards we are called to uphold may at times seem hard to bear, but with Christ's help, we can overcome and be victorious. I came across this article on crosswalk.com titled "12 Ways Satan May Try to Destroy You, Pastor"[41] (adapted from the book *A Puritan Theology: Doctrine for Life*).[42] It lists 12 devices Satan uses to destroy pastors as catalogued by William Spurstowe. However, I would like to share nine of them with you. It would behoove us all to pay close attention to these and stay alert and cognizant of the devil's schemes. They are:

Device 1: "Satan leads men from lesser sins to greater. People usually think of lesser sins as nothing more serious than a cold. But Spurstowe warned, 'Small sins are as the priming of a post or pillar that prepare it to better receive those other colours that are to be laid upon it.' Small sins leach away our fear of God and hatred of sin. Remedy: 'Take heed of giving place to the devil.' (Ephesians 4:27 NIV). If you let the serpent's head into your house, his whole body will quickly follow."

Device 2: "The devil persistently urges men to a particular sin. He inserts evil thoughts in the mind. (John 13:2 NIV). He persistently presses until men succumb, as Delilah did with Samson. (Judges 16:16 NIV). Remedy: Reject the promises of sin.... For those who prefer peace with sin rather than war against the devil, Rutherford wrote, 'The devil's war is better than the devil's peace.'"

Device 3: "Satan makes a strategic retreat for a time to draw us out of our position of strength...he permits us a momentary victory to 'swell the heart with pride.' Remedy: "Christians in this world should not live like rich men in a king's court but like soldiers in the camps of war."

Device 4: "'Satan clothes evil with false appearances.' (Isaiah 5:20 NLT). He dyes sin with the colours of virtue so that greed becomes frugality, and lukewarmness appears to be moderation. Remedy: We must love the truth of the Bible. 'Truth is the food of the soul,' Spurstowe said. Brooks said, 'A man may lawfully sell his house, land, and jewels, but truth is a jewel that exceeds all price, and must not be sold.'"

Device 5: "Satan ensnares men with lawful things. With this ploy, a quiet stream will carry more boats over the waterfall than noisy rapids. Richard Gilpin (1625-1700) said that 'worldly delights' are 'Satan's great engine' of temptation.' Remedy: Spurstowe urged caution in the use of things that might prove to be temptations… 'Our hearts are [gun] powder, and therefore we must take heed of sparks.'"

Device 6: "The demons surprise or shock people with temptations. They make them think no one else has experienced such temptations before. Remedy: Spurstowe wrote, 'Suspect yourself prone to every sin; do not repose anything on constitution or temperament.'"

Device 7: "Satan attacks the conscience and assurance of believers with false reasoning. He might use a false syllogism such as, 'This sin cannot remain in a true child of God. But it remains in you. Therefore, you are not a true child of God.' Remedy: Spurstowe said true conversion is not determined by whether sin remains in us, but whether sin *reigns* in us."

Device 8: "The tempter entices people with the promise that they can repent easily after sinning. Remedy: Repentance is a mighty work, a difficult work, a work that is above our power. Repentance is a great grace from God."

Device 9: "Satan drives men from one extreme to the other. He pushes believers' pendulum from presumptuous sin to despair over sin, and from neglect of religious duties to 'such a rigorous tyranny that makes many to groan under them.' Remedy: Spurstowe said, 'Faith leaves both extremes and closes with [embraces] God according to the rule of the Word.'"

1 Timothy 3:1-7 lays out for us the standards and behavioural expectations of pastors and leaders. In verse two, the phrase "above reproach" has been commonly used to remind pastors of what is expected of us as spiritual leaders. This phrase, which aims at our private and public behaviour, means "...proven, observable conduct that is blameless in marital life, family life, social life, and business life."[43] Both the #MeToo and the #ChurchToo movements have come along to remind us and hold us accountable to the biblical and denominational standards that we have endeavoured to live by. In all our human frailties, let us determine that we will represent Christ to the best of our ability and so sustain the respect and credibility that is associated with the office of the clergy.

FOR REFLECTION AND INTROSPECTION

1. What is your opinion on the #MeToo and #ChurchToo movements? What did they teach you about the times we are living in? Did they inspire you to make any changes in your life?

2. Did it shock you to see the statistics on pastors? If you are in a Christian leadership position, how can you

ensure that you live a life that is above reproach? If you are a congregant, how does this report change the way you pray for your pastors?

3. Given the devices that Satan uses, what can you do to ensure that you do not fall into his trap?

Chapter 5

LEARNING FROM DAVID

"...I have found David son of Jesse a man after my
own heart; he will do everything I want him to do."

Acts 13:22 NIV

YOU KNOW YOU are a candidate to receive God's grace, mercy,
and unfailing love when you derive comfort from the words
and life of a murderer and adulterer. Some of my close friends
and colleagues must have seen a correlation between David's
sin and mine, because they all recommended that I go back
and read and reflect on Psalm 51. I took their advice. Shortly
after my public confession, I took the better part of a month
and memorized all 19 verses of this Psalm. At this stage of
my life, this turned out to be quite a gruelling exercise. Verses
did not stick the way they did when I was a child. But this
was, nonetheless, a good exercise, even though a year later I
had forgotten most of it. But among other benefits, it served
to renew and refocus my mind on the Word, as opposed to
being consumed by what I imagined many were saying about
me and the trust I sensed I had lost. Reading this Psalm of
repentance also gave me comfort and liberation during my

season of remorse. The most comforting and intriguing truth I especially cherished about David's life was that though he was an adulterer and a murderer, at the end of his life, God gave David one of the highest commendations He has given to anyone. He described His servant David as "a man after My own heart."

My True Confession

Margaret Singleton and Ray Stevens are the lyricists of the song "My True Confession".[44] In 1961, Brook Benton's rendition of this classic song ended up selling a record-breaking number of "45s" that decade. Regardless of how real, true, or sincere the words of the song are, those who love the song probably feel that way because of the creativity expressed by the suitor to make a last desperate plea to regain the love and trust of his partner. To ensure that his message gets to her untainted, the suitor petitions the editor of a make-believe magazine to publish, and hence make public, his "true confession." You can almost hear the sincerity in his tone through his poetic words. There is a desperate urgency sounded as he determines to make the wrongs he has committed right. If you are from the Boomer Generation, you would most likely know this song and recall the opening plea of the song writers:

> Dear Mr. Editor, wontcha please
> Print my story in your magazine?
> Warn all the lovers how a cheating heart
> Can only end up in misery.

Feel free to check out the rest of the words of this song. But my main reason for taking you down memory lane is simply to make this comparison: At the end of the day, at the end of the song, at the end of that trip down lover's lane, at the end of his intimate relationship (inferred), Singleton's "true confession" pales against David's in Psalm 51. This Psalm has become my standard for what true confession looks like. It frees us of all sham and insincerity. It encourages us to make ministry a safe place as we confess and repent of our sins. But for true confession to happen, we need to first face the gravity of our sinful heart. David did this in this Psalm.

Among the Old Testament devotees, David, I believe, emerges as a favourite hero/biblical character in the minds of many of us. I specifically like David because he lived an authentic life. From a young boy tending his father's sheep, right up to the writing of his last Psalm, there is a realness in his life's journey. Some of the tough lessons he had to learn caused him to be honest, transparent, humble, and contrite. Here in this prayer for restoration, David asks God for favour, mercy, forgiveness, and cleansing. Out of a broken spirit, he confesses and accepts full responsibility for his sin.

I have always been intrigued and a bit awestruck whenever I have reflected on God's approbation of David. When you read of David's well-known sins and then place them against the backdrop of God's commentary on him, it almost seems as though it does not add up. It's as though the commendation is some sort of mistake on God's part. But I have since given it some thought and have concluded that one of the reasons why God referred to David as "a man after his own heart" (1 Samuel 13:14 NLT) was because David was always willing to humbly repent of his sins. He was careful to return to God to repair his broken relationship with Him.

I believe David knew he had a strong propensity to sin, but with the same intensity, he was quick to offer his sincere repentance to God. This was quite a humbling and genuine quality David possessed. I don't know how many of us, having been exposed after committing gross sins like adultery and murder, would have the courage to come back and ask for forgiveness. David did. Over and over again. This is why I am greatly helped and encouraged by Psalm 51. It has, among other things, a calm, reassuring, restorative feel to it. Now as a fallen servant of God, I too find myself reinvigorated by it and take solace in the fact that when God looks at my sinful life, He administers a similar kind of grace.

My moral failure and its revelation to everyone have given me a fresh appreciation for David's honesty and open confession in Psalm 51. In times past, as I read the Psalms of David, I empathized with him as he poured out his heart and soul before God. But today I have a personal identity with what he might have felt and experienced.

What follows is my personal identity with David's sin of adultery and the commentary that a few of my favourite bible scholars have made about this Psalm. Of course, this annotation of Psalm 51 is a far cry from exhausting all the truths embodied in it, but my hope is that it will, at least, spur you on to do a deeper study of this fabulous song.

The ensuing thoughts that I would like to share are intended for spiritual rejuvenation, and would be especially helpful for small-group discussions. My prayer is that as group members pore over the truths expressed in Psalm 51, they would live them out and experience, among other take-a-ways, a strong resolve to take preventative measures to avoid committing the sin of adultery.

The Bible version I have chosen to use is the New Living Translation.

Chapter Outline

Over the decades, several well-thought-out outlines of this Psalm have been offered by scholars. But for simplicity sake, I have chosen to utilize the Psalm division that commentator Ray Pritchard[45] used:

> Confession: Verses 1-6
> Cleansing: Verses 7-12
> Consecration: Verses 13-19

In the first section, David confesses his sin. In the second section, he petitions God to remove his guilt and cleanse him inwardly. In the third section, he recommits himself to a life-style of joy and wisdom in the service of God and others.

Now as we work our way through this Psalm, if you have never done this before, try to feel the magnitude of David's sin. Hear the broken sobs vividly expressed: Have mercy! Cleanse! Blot out! Wash! Purge! Hide your face from my sins! Create! Do not cease! Renew! Restore! Save! Open my lips! Wow! What honesty and sincerity of heart David displays in this Psalm! Understand clearly that how we respond when we have sinned reveals a great deal about the reality or unreality of our profession of faith. It is therefore with total contriteness of heart that David offers this confession.

Confession: Verses 1-6

> Verse 1: "Have mercy on me, O God, because of your unfailing love. Because of your great compassion, blot out the stain of my sins."

Mercy is so applicable to this plea, for without it, we are totally and finally ruined and undone. The old saying states that confession is good for the soul. That is true! Confession has the power to change everything in our circumstances. Andy Stanley articulates it this way: "It breaks the power of the enemy off of you as your situation is no longer a secret. It empowers you to settle your outstanding debts with others, God, and even yourself. Removing the debt-to-debtor dynamic from a relationship paves the way to better relationship, understanding, and openness. Confession allows us to come out of hiding."[46]

Once we acknowledge our helplessness and dependence on God, real change can occur. Then we can take the next step and confess our sins to God. This is why acting on God's promise in 1 John 1:9 is of crucial importance: "If we confess our sins, he is faithful and just and will forgive us our sins and purify us from all unrighteousness." Titus 2:14 reminds us why this is true. Christ "...gave himself for us to redeem us from all wickedness and to purify for himself a people that are his very own, eager to do what is good."

"Have mercy on me, O God...is a prayer of a man who knows he has sinned and is deprived of all self-justification."[47] This is a marvellous understanding of the nature of sin. It requires God's mercy, and David appeals for this. This opening plea lets those of us who have sinned greatly and are overwhelmed by feelings of guilt know that God is willing to forgive us if we honestly cry out to Him. David's plea in this opening verse is a fitting place to start.

He begins by crying out for God's mercy, love, and compassion. He seriously wants to put as much distance as possible between himself and his sins. It is his way of saying the time for excuses is over. He cannot afford to be trivial about such grave sins like adultery and murder. Moreover, as long as a man makes excuses, he cannot be forgiven because he will not come clean about his sin. If we feel the need to justify our sin, we are not ready for forgiveness. Rather, like David, we need to plead for a cleansing from God, and in confessing our sin, we appeal to God's forgiving character.

According to J. Sanders, the author of *Enjoying Intimacy with God*, "The concept behind the Greek word for confess is 'to say the same thing'—it is to admit oneself to be guilty of what one is charged with." He goes on to say, "When we confess our sin and acknowledge our guilt to God, we agree with Him in His assessment of the seriousness of our sin and take sides with Him against it."[48] When we confess our sin, we own it. And when we confess and repent, we become safe for ministry.

Sanders expresses it this way: "In asking God to blot out the stain of my (our) sins, we are in essence saying, 'Erase and obliterate them so completely that not a trace remains.' For David, forgiveness was not sufficient if it left him still with a burden of guilt, and a sense of defilement. The intolerable weight must be lifted and the pollution removed—hence the reason for the plea to completely do away with his sin."[49] Clarke renders the interpretation of "blot out" this way: "As is the case with all ink stains, David is here asking …that a proper fluid be applied to the parchment, to discharge the ink, that no record of it may ever appear against him: and this only the mercy, lovingkindness, and tender compassions of the Lord can do."[50]

Sin, David understands, is an illegal act, a violation of justice, an act of lawlessness and rebellion and, therefore, requires mercy.[51] David shows here a debilitating remorse over sin that can only be eased in true confession. He recognizes that his sin is inexcusable; it is like an ugly stain, a defilement upon the soul. Even though the act fades into the past, the dirty defiling stains remain a stigma upon the heart. He felt so polluted by his sins that he asked again and again for cleansing. Where we may be tempted or prone to shift the responsibility of our sins from ourselves to others, David takes full responsibility.

It is clearly evident that David truly understands the nature of sin and the heart of his God to forgive. Consequently, he asks for forgiveness on the basis of two things: 1.) God's unfailing love. This is because he is cognizant of the fact that he deserves nothing from God and that He is not bound to forgive him.[52] 2.) God's great compassion. In so doing, he is appealing to God's promise in Exodus 34:6-7: "…The Lord, the Lord, a God merciful and gracious, slow to anger and abounding in steadfast love and faithfulness, keeping steadfast love for thousands, forgiving iniquity and transgression and sin, but who will by no means clear the guilty…." Understanding this type of generosity from God, David feels he will be forgiven beyond his utmost imagination.

> Verse 2: "Wash me clean from my guilt. Purify me from my sin."

This request clearly reveals that David felt dirty and stained by his sin. He equates sin to an ugly stain, a defilement of the soul. By asking to be washed clean, he is inferring that his sin stain is deep, and an ordinary purification will not be sufficient. Steadman says, "Even though the act fades into the past, the dirty defiling stain remains a stigma upon the heart."[53] Though he lived in this condition for some time (bible scholars estimate it was approximately one year), David did not have full knowledge of his iniquity and sin. But now the "stain" of his sin has weighed him down.[54] So much so that he pleads for a thorough washing and purifying of his guilt and sin—the type of job only God can do. No one and nothing else can do it more effectively. The thoroughness of this washing implies a cleansing, not just from outward defilement, but from an inner bent to sin.

> Verse 3: "For I recognize my rebellion; it haunts me day and night."

What honesty! In this statement, David genuinely confesses his sin, the condition of his heart, and the state of his conscience. These are the words of a genuinely remorseful person. I love the way Eugene Peterson, in *The Message*, paraphrases this verse: "I know how bad I have been, my sins are staring me down." The solution to his and our dilemma can only be found in the forgiveness offered by a loving God. The Holy Spirit has brought David to the place where he realizes his heart needs a renovation. David's conscience is alive and actively at work, so much so, that he cannot get this sin off of his mind. It is always before him. His sin, not just the consequences, haunts him by day and disrupts his sleep by night. His mind keeps rehearsing it as if it were a song on a CD player programmed on repeat. Sadly, I also know this feeling all too well! It is what I call the monthly payments for sin after a small deposit was made for the transgression. It is important to note that if the process of forgiveness is to happen, sin has to be called what it is: sin. Sin is not a "problem", "a weakness", or an "unguarded moment". No. Sin is missing God's mark.

The Holy Spirit had worked such an acute sense of sin in David's heart that he employed the use of three words to reinforce this point: 1.) *Guilt* (or transgression), which conveys an overstepping of God-given boundaries and an admission to the breaking of God's law; 2.) *Rebellion* (or iniquity) to describe that which is off the straight path and is now on the morally crooked path; and (3) *Sin,* which is failing to reach the divine standard and goal.[55] In the months between the time

David committed these sins and his confession, he could not escape the sense of sin—it was always before him. He did his best to ignore it and deny it, but as a genuine child of God, he could not escape it. He was living in a state of unconfessed sin, but miserable in it, as any Christian should be.[56]

It is interesting to note that David did not say, "My punishment is ever before me" or "My consequences are ever before me." What bothered him was his sin. Many grieve over the consequences of sin, few over sin itself.[57] Unfortunately, I too have been guilty of this fact. Here again, by taking ownership of his sin, David is accepting full responsibility for his wrongdoing. I have found that this is the best way of setting the stage for genuine forgiveness and healing.

> Verse 4: "Against you, and you alone, have I sinned: I have done what is evil in your sight. You will be proved right in what you say, and your judgment against me is just."

We all struggle with our sinful nature, which unfortunately lives in us even after we are born again! Butterfield reminds us of this truth: "Sin is treason, not sinus trouble. God forgives sin; he does not heal sin."[58] Once we have recognized we have sinned against Him, we should admit it and seek His forgiveness and restoration.

Clarke feels that depending on the way this verse is translated, it could or could not be applicable to David's sin with Bathsheba. But assuming it is, David is making a very definitive statement here. In honesty and sincerity, he is not intentionally overlooking the fact that he has sinned against Uriah, Bathsheba, the people of Israel, and even his own body. (1 Corinthians 6:18). This is a hyperbole, as David knows he also sinned against several other people. But here he owns up to the fact that the person most offended by his sin is God. His offence against God is most disturbing, and he expects God to rebuke him and hand down whatever verdict He sees fit.

"You're the One I have violated, and you have seen it all, seen the full extent of my evil." (*The Message,* v. 4). For all sin is treason against God. In David's case, he knew that his sin affected not just him, but the whole nation! Until we grasp this, until we see it and feel it, until we confess it, we cannot be forgiven.[59] Actually, what makes sin extremely sinful is that it is against God. Hurting humans is bad and horrible, but the real atrocity is that sin is an attack on and a belittling of God![60]

David realizes this is no private sin, and therefore, the idea of trying to cover his tracks will no longer work. So, he comes clean and confesses. He is aware of the fact that he can no longer escape the social consequences of his fall. This fresh insight into the nature of sin enabled David to admit that God is proved right in everything He says, and therefore, His judgment and verdict for him must be accepted. Notice there is no self-justification, no defense, and no escape, because God is just and is free to mete out the harshest punishment to him. In fact, David "confirms God's justice and holy character, proving that His commands were good and just even when David broke those commands."[61]

David's thoughts conjure up the picture that God was there and fully aware of what he was doing when he committed this evil. What a reminder to us that God is not absent from the bedroom or place where the adultery is committed and where subsequent sins are done.[62]

> Verse 5: "For I was born a sinner—yes, from the moment my mother conceived me."

The first time I read this verse I liked it because it reminded me that all humans are born sinners, having received a sinful nature from our parents Adam and Eve. I liked it because I thought it helped me to justify my sin and to diminish my personal guilt. But it didn't take too long for me to realize I was wrong. I wanted to interpret this verse my way and use it as an excuse to reveal that from the outset of my birth, I started life at a disadvantage. While there might have been some truth there, this is not what David is saying here. He is not making excuses for his sin, but rather identifies with this universal human condition. The real purpose for this statement was to "show the depths of his sin, that it went beyond specific sinful actions all the way to a stubborn sin nature, one he was born with;"[63] but not one that left him incapable of rising above his bent.

We also clearly understand that David was not casting blame on his mother by inferring he was born out of a sinful relationship. No. Rather, he was actually referring to the biblical teaching of original sin, in which we humans are born sinners by virtue of the sinful nature of our parents Adam and Eve.[64] He was acknowledging here that from his infancy, he possessed a natural propensity to sin. He was, in essence, confirming what Galatians 5:16-17, 19-21 state about our sinful nature. David was here "…indicating he now saw that his outward crimes were only the expression of his inveterately (old) sinful nature." What David was actually saying is this: "…the act of conception introduced him into a sinful humanity, that he was born into a sinful race in which sin was already deeply imbedded." According to Steadman, it is as if David was saying, "I see now that sin is not just a surface problem that can be handled lightly; it is a deep problem. It has stained my whole nature. Unless I find some solution for this polluted nature, I will never be able to keep from falling back into sin again."[65]

So in essence, what David is acknowledging here is that his acts of adultery, murder, and lying are expressions of something worse! He is by nature a sinner! If God does not rescue him, he will do more and more evil. All this comes as a stark reminder to us that sin is so deeply ingrained in us that it cannot be cured by anything but the substitutional death of our Lord and Saviour on the cross.

> Verse 6: "But you desire honesty from the womb, teaching me wisdom even there."

This is David's way of saying that God wants to have truth and honesty as foundational qualities in our lives. This should start in the womb. Guzik explains it this way: "Though the sin nature was deep within David, God wanted to work deeply in him. God wanted a transformation in David all the way to the inward parts, to the hidden part that would know wisdom."[66] By making reference all the way back to the womb, David is saying he does not need a superficial reform, but rather something much deeper. He is saying, "…help me to understand the truth about myself, that I am a fallen being and that this pollution has penetrated my whole nature."[67] Even though God had been his teacher and had blessed him with so much wisdom and knowledge, sin had gotten the upper hand on him. So by recognizing what God really desires, he also confesses the depth of his corruption.

Pritchard makes an interesting observation about "truth" per this verse in the New International Version: "Surely you desire truth in the inner parts." He claims that our problem is not one of hearing or knowing more truth, but rather needing to allow the "incoming bullets of truth" to get close enough to us to hurt us. In strengthening his points, he says this: "When David cried out for God's mercy, he acknowledged the true source of the problem and where the healing must begin. Until there is 'truth'…in the inner recesses of the soul, as long as we lie to ourselves, we can never get better, and God cannot teach us wisdom."[68]

Cleansing: Verses 7-12

Verse 7: "Purify me from my sins, and I will be clean; wash me, and I will be whiter than snow."

In other versions, this phrase is stated: "Cleanse me with hyssop," (NIV) or "Purge me with hyssop," (KJV) or stated more contemporarily: "Soak me in your laundry, and I'll come out clean, scrub me, and I'll have a snow-white life." (*The Message,* v. 7). Whichever version you prefer, the intent of David was clear. He wanted to have his sin completely purged away. Commentators agree that David is here alluding to the cleansing that is done with the sacrificial blood of animals that was required for the defilement of a person (or thing) to be removed. In other words, atonement by death must be made to eradicate the guilt from a sinner. "Purge me", for example, is based on the word for sin (*chattath*) and literally means "de-sin me" or "take away the mass of sin." And why hyssop? Hyssop was a plant used in the first Passover in Egypt. (Exodus 12:22). The Jews dipped the hyssop in the blood of the lamb and then smeared the blood on the doorpost. As a result of this exercise, on that historical night, when the angel of death saw the blood, he "passed over" that house and no one died.

Today, of course, Christ is our Passover Lamb whose blood washes away our sin. (1 Corinthians 5:7; 1 John 1:7).[69] In essence, David realized that God couldn't just improve his old life or make it better; He couldn't just cleanse it. No. He needed to put it to death. Steadman articulates it this way: "In understanding the gravity of his sin, David says to God, 'If you are going to deal with this terrible fountain of evil in me, I can see that it must be put to death. It must be purged with hyssop, then I will be clean.'"[70] The imagery is so beautiful here. David shows the stark contrast between the red stain of blood and the white cleanliness of snow. This is what God's purging/washing of us produces.

> Verse 8: "Oh, give me back my joy again; you have broken me—now let me rejoice."

Regaining our joy is a gracious gift from God, and when we feel totally broken, this gift becomes very precious. In commenting on the statement, "Make me to hear joy," Clarke shares these thoughts: "Let me have a full testimony of my reconciliation to thee: that the soul which is so deeply distressed by a sense of thy displeasure, may be healed by a sense of thy pardoning mercy."[71] This is what a sinful heart needs most, and David has clearly made his request known.

Isn't it interesting that David does not give any credit to the enemy for his fall? No, he knows that it is God who permits everything to happen to us. David understands that the same God who has broken him has the propensity to make him rejoice again. The brokenness that David felt was fitting for a sinner under the conviction of the Holy Spirit. And being confident that this was the work of the Holy Spirit, David could pray that it would lead to joy and gladness; that out of his brokenness he would rejoice. The restoration of joy is what he longs for, and God is always willing to restore the broken. Forgiven people are committed to being changed by God.

> Verse 9: "Don't keep looking at my sins. Remove the stain of my guilt."

In *The Message* (v. 9), the verse is paraphrased this way: "Do not look too close for blemishes, give me a clean bill of health." Steadman interprets this verse like this: "Father, if I am going to be able to be free from falling again, then something has got to be done about the past. I can't always be having it thrown up to me forever. That only depresses me and discourages me, and if I am going to have to live with my wretched, miserable past, I will be defeated over and over again. So God, I am asking you, hide your face from my sins and blot out my iniquity." What a realistic way of paraphrasing this verse!

> Verse 10: "Create in me a clean heart, O God. Renew a loyal spirit within me."

The verb "create" is such a suitable one to use here. David looks to God, and God alone, for a heart cleansing. He understands that all the self-help measures he would be tempted to employ will not change him. He knows that his heart is altogether so corrupt that a patch-up job will not suffice here. It must be made new—as it was in the beginning. In other words, he needs God's creating or recreating work to be done to his heart. Coupled with this request, David asks for a loyal spirit, a steadfast spirit, a right spirit. This is the kind of grace that is really needed to counteract the sin of adultery and all other vile sins committed against God.

Isn't it interesting that nowhere in his prayer does David directly plead with God to help him with sexual sin? Notice he does not ask for sexual restraint. He doesn't pray for protected eyes and sex-free thoughts. As a matter of fact, he doesn't even pray for men to hold him accountable. After all, we all know these are crucial areas in which we need God's divine help. But like us, David knows that sexual sin is symptomatic of a much greater problem. And in this prayer, David shows us who have sinned sexually what our real need is. We have a "heart" problem. This is why when we are enticed, we give way because God does not have the rightful place in our hearts and thoughts.[72] Only God can create or renovate our hearts to bring them into alignment with His will for us. This I pray for all of my readers.

> Verse 11: "Do not banish me from your presence, and don't take your Holy Spirit from me."

This is a petition for intimacy with God. For me, feeling God's presence and the conviction work of His Spirit were the first signs of spiritual healing and a reconnecting with Him. I became aware of the fact that: "Only the power of the Holy Spirit can change the human will to make it loyal and willing to obey."[73] My prayer was: "Do not throw me out with the trash or fail to breathe holiness in me." (*The Message*, v. 11). Here, David might have been thinking about Saul's fear of being cast away when the Spirit of God departed from him. (1 Samuel 16:14). That's an awful place to be! To be cast away from God's presence is synonymous with experiencing the end of your relationship with Him. Moses understood this dynamic when he prayed: "If your presence doesn't go with us, do not send us up from here." (Exodus 33:15 NIV). For, as the Psalmist says, in His presence there is fullness of joy and at His right hand, pleasures forever more. (Psalm 16:11).

> Verse 12: "Restore to me the joy of your salvation, and make me willing to obey you."

When we experience the loss of God's presence and the power of His Holy Spirit, these are signs that something needs to be re-established. For David it was his joy and obedience. Every sin separates us from the happy fellowship and closeness we had with God. The solution? We need to regain the delight of

God's salvation. With every passing day, David felt the misery of spiritual defeat. He longed to experience once again the joy that accompanies salvation. As can be expected, God did restore to David the joy of His salvation. However, the rest of David's life reminds us that God does not save us from the consequences of sin. Regardless of how sincere our repentance and confessions are, there are penalties to our sin. And this truth is sometimes realized too late!

Consecration: Verses 13-19

> Verse 13: "Then I will teach your ways to rebels, and they will return to you."

This verse especially resonates with me because one of my gifts is teaching, coupled with a passion to see the lost come to Christ. The hope expressed in this verse encourages me and reminds me of a similar promise God gave to Peter in Luke 22:31-32: "Simon, Simon, Satan has asked to sift each of you like wheat. But I have pleaded in prayer for you, Simon, that your faith should not fail. So when you have repented and turned to me again, strengthen your brothers."

Like Simon, I believe God will use me again, especially to help those who are struggling with habitual sin and guilt and have lost hope in God. I believe out of my brokenness, many will experience wholeness and return to Him. Having experienced restoration, I want to see similar sinners led in the same direction. I concur with Pritchard when he says: "Converted sinners make the best preachers because they know the truth of what they are saying."[74] I want to use that which Satan intended to shipwreck my ministry to be the very tool God uses to bring others back to Himself. I am the recipient of God's pardoning grace and mercy, and I want to be gracious and merciful to others in return. I want my testimony to be a breath of fresh air to those "rebels" who have given up on God.

> Verse 14: "Forgive me for shedding blood, O God who saves; then I will joyfully sing of your forgiveness."

This idiom of "shedding blood" includes any injustice, not just homicide. Here, David is serious about once again joyfully singing, knowing that he has been freed from his horrific sins. Nowhere in the Psalm is he concerned about escaping the material consequences of his sins: It is the guilt of them that burdens him. Even deliverance is too narrow a word; in reality he wants to praise God's righteousness. In this verse, David considers the fact that the blood of Uriah…"cries for vengeance against him; and nothing but the mere mercy of God can wipe this blood from his conscience."[75]

> Verse 15: "Unseal my lips, O Lord, that my mouth may praise you."

Sin has a way of not just separating us from God, but also of shutting down our testimony. We feel as if our worship is empty and void of the Holy Spirit's presence, so we struggle to enter into a private or corporate worship experience. Added to this fact is that we no longer feel qualified to share the Word with others. The enemy convinces us that our witness will fall on unresponsive hearts. So we seal our lips. This part of David's prayer is therefore a "cry of one whose conscience has shamed him into silence." "His lips were shut until grace like a river came pouring down from heaven."[76] The takeaway from this verse is simply this: Truly forgiven people will delight in telling others what God has done for them. They move quickly from sealed lips to satisfying worship.

Verse 16-17: "You do not desire a sacrifice, or I would offer one. You do not want a burnt offering. The sacrifice you desire is a broken spirit. You will not reject a broken and repentant heart, O God."

Pritchard shares that: "These verses banish forever the false notion that God wants more religion." He goes on to say this: "In the old days, it was the blood of bulls and goats. In modern times, it is church attendance and money in the offering plate. You can go to church for a thousand Sundays in a row and it would not remove the stain of even one sin. David knew that no bull offered on the altar could ever atone for the sins of murder and adultery. What God wants is a broken and contrite heart."[77] Understand this: The best of gifts is hateful to God without a repentant heart. In other words, God is looking for the heart that knows how little it deserves and how much it owes. One commentator makes this observation: "A person having a broken spirit loses his vital life energy; his entire disposition has been humbled under the mighty hand of God." Piper enhances this thought with this truth: "Being broken and contrite is not against joy and praise and witness. It's the flavour of Christian joy and praise and witness."[78]

Watchman Nee, in his book entitled, *The Normal Christian Life*, illustrated the concept of brokenness to a young Christian brother. One day while they were having supper and discussing the topic of natural energy, the young man said this to him: "It is a blessed thing when you know the Lord has met you and touched you…and that disabling touch has been received." In response, Nee picked up a biscuit off of the plate on the table between them and broke it in half as if he intended to eat it. Then, fitting the two pieces together again carefully, he said this: "It looks all right, but it is never quite going to be the same again, is it? When once your back is broken, you will yield ever after to the slightest touch from God."[79] Indeed! Such is the nature of one whose spirit has been broken by God. They never trust in themselves again!

> Verse 18: "Look with favour on Zion and help her; rebuild the walls of Jerusalem."

David speaks here of Zion's spiritual plight in physical terms. He admits that his sin has had a negative impact on the whole nation. Consequently, Zion needs God's help. They all need God to heal their hurts and to secure and protect them against the attack of enemies due to their broken-down walls. But David is conscious of the fact that his whole nation is in jeopardy because of his sin. "The very walls (a symbol of security) are under attack because of the evil that he has done."[80]

All over North America today, indeed all over the world, societies are suffering from the sins of adultery, sexual immorality, pornography, etc. It therefore behoves us to pray, like David, for God to once again look with favour on us and rebuild the spiritual walls and fabric of our lives. We desperately need His favour today. Then we will see God restore us to the place where we ought to be spiritually.

> Verse 19: "Then you will be pleased with sacrifices offered in the right spirit—with burnt offerings and whole burnt offerings. Then bulls will again be sacrificed on your altar."

"Then worship will be realistic. It will be offered in 'spirit and in truth'. Every song sung, every Psalm read, every prayer uttered will not be a mechanical perfunctory repetition of words but the healthy articulation of a heart that has been cleansed and set free."[81]

The foregone comments on this powerful Psalm are but a few thoughts expressed by way of commentary. However, it is my prayer that as we reflect on these truths and determine to put them into practice, we will experience God's restorative love and healing to our souls.

A Word of Caution

Maybe you have been reading this commentary on Psalm 51, and you found it hard to relate to because the sins of adultery and murder are not temptations that assail you. While as human beings we fall into the habit of categorizing sin into various levels of seriousness, in the eyes of God, sin is sin. Whether it's something as "small" as a little white lie, or it's something as "big" as murder, all sin is offensive to God. If there is one thing we can learn from the outpouring of David's heart in Psalm 51, it's that: "All sin ruptures fellowship, destroys intimacy with God, produces a sense of guilt, and involves the sinning person in painful temporal and eternal loss."[82]

"If we claim to be without sin, we deceive ourselves and the truth is not in us. If we confess our sins, he is faithful and just and will forgive us our sins and purify us from all unrighteousness." (1 John 1:8-9 NIV).

Back in the fall of 2017, Pastor J.D. Mallory preached a message he entitled "Mooing Cows and Bleating Sheep".[83] During this sermon, the Holy Spirit convicted me of sin and the need for confession. I was reminded of a truth that gripped my heart and transformed my thoughts and lifestyle that morning. One of the points he developed was as follows: While a 97% mark would be accepted as an excellent grade one may ascribe to their spiritual standing with God, it still does not constitute an A+ in the eyes of the Lord! Why? Simply because God requires 100% of our obedience. The missing 3% is due to the fact that there is still an area of sin or stronghold in our life that we have chosen not to surrender to Him. Consequently, we are only as strong as our secrets. And God does not accept our corporate worship on Sunday when He knows that on Monday we will continue to sin against Him.

I believe the Holy Spirit wanted to make abundantly clear to me, and probably many other parishioners that morning, that like Saul, we have deliberately chosen to keep some "choice sheep and cattle" for our own pleasure. (Read 1 Samuel 15:1-26 for the fuller context of this thought.) But God's bottom line is this: Honestly confess and turn away from all sin.

Sure, we ought to be proud of our 97% spiritual accomplishments, while at the same time being careful of at least two things: 1.) We do not adopt the self-righteous attitude of the Pharisee who prayed: "God, I thank you I am not like other men—robbers, evildoers, adulterers—or even like this tax collector." (Luke 18:11b NIV). The 3% spirituality he lacked was evidenced by his prideful boasting of his achievements, thus rendering his 97% righteousness null and void! 2.) God still looks at our heart; not our man-made spiritual track record.

So let me conclude on the same sobering note as David when he began his confession: "Have mercy on me, O God, because of your unfailing love. Because of your great compassion, blot out the stain of my sins." (Psalm 51:1 NLT).

FOR REFLECTION AND INTROSPECTION

1. In what area(s) are you particularly susceptible to temptation? If not adultery, what is your unique sin

bent? Do you believe that God is able to deliver you from this bondage? Why not ask Him to?

2. When and where do you face temptations? How can you seek God's wisdom and help in turning away from them?

3. Have you ever felt like your sin is so bad, and you have been indulging in it for so long that even God can't rid you of it? That a common lie the devil uses. Don't buy into it. Honestly confess your sin and trust God to keep you from going back into it.

Chapter 6

RENEWED BY HIS LOVE

"This is love: not that we loved God, but that he loved us
and sent his Son as an atoning sacrifice for our sins."

1 John 4:10 NIV

ON ONE OCCASION when I was preaching on the well-known
story of the Prodigal Son,[84] by way of introduction, I asked
the congregation: "What comes to mind when you hear the
word 'prodigal'?" True to form, their responses to the perceived
meaning of the word were all the same and exactly what I
had expected. "Wayward" was the popular answer. "Renegade"
brought a good second. Other suggestions were "disobedient",
"irresponsible", "bad", etc. The reason why their answers did
not surprise me was because I also held a similar view of the
meaning of the word until I reflected on a brilliant piece of
work written by one of my favourite authors, Timothy Keller,
entitled, *The Prodigal God.*[85] To my embarrassment, I have
always associated wayward behaviour with the word "prodigal"; and so the title of Keller's book immediately caught my
attention. After reading it, I was edified, blessed, convicted,

and felt like I owed my past congregants an apology for giving an erroneous treatment of this parable.

Prodigal God

In the introduction of this book, Keller clarified for me, and I'm sure a few of my present readers, the meaning of the word "prodigal". "The word 'prodigal'," he says, "does not mean 'wayward' but, according to the Merriam-Webster's Collegiate Dictionary, 'recklessly spendthrift'. It means to spend until you have nothing left. The term is therefore as appropriate for describing the father in the story as it is for his younger son. The father's welcome to the repentant son was literally reckless, because he refused to 'reckon' or count his sin against him or demand repayment."[86]

This gave me much hope as a sinner myself and one who can be placed in a category Keller calls "The Lost Younger Brother", as opposed to "The Lost Elder Brother". [87] Interestingly enough, one of the truths taught in this parable is the fact that both brothers missed God: the younger brother broke the rules and missed God; and the older brother followed the rules and missed God as well. Identifying with the younger brother's behaviour, I was reminded that my Father still loves me even though, at times, I also serve Him for the wrong reasons.

In the earlier part of 2018, while going through my restoration journey, the popular Christian song "Reckless Love", written by Cory Asbury, Caleb Culver, and Ran Jackson, was introduced as one of the new worship songs in our church. I was again struck by the title and immediately felt drawn to the words of this song. For those who may not be familiar with this song, I have included most of the words of the song below. For the complete words of the song, you may want to pull it up on Google or YouTube. And while you are at it, why not listen to it and be blessed?

I don't how many lives have been touched and encouraged and regained hope and experienced God's love through the words of this song. But for me, these words resonated in my heart at a time when I needed to be reminded about how God feels about me.

Reckless Love[88]

Before I spoke a word, You were singing over me
You have been so, so good to me
Before I took a breath, You breathed Your life in me
You have been so, so kind to me

O, the overwhelming, never-ending, reckless love
of God
O, it chases me down, fights 'til I'm found, leaves
the ninety-nine
I couldn't earn it, and I don't deserve it, still, You give
Yourself away
O, the overwhelming, never-ending, reckless love of
God, yeah

When I was Your foe, still Your love fought for me
You have been so, so good to me
When I felt no worth, You paid it all for me
You have been so, so kind to me

O, the overwhelming, never-ending, reckless love
of God
O, it chases me down, fights 'til I'm found, leaves
the ninety-nine
I couldn't earn it, and I don't deserve it, still, You give
Yourself away

O, the overwhelming, never-ending, reckless love of
God, yeah

There's no shadow You won't light up
Mountain You won't climb up
Coming after me
There's no wall You won't kick down
Lie You won't tear down
Coming after me

I was particularly blessed when I reflected on the imagery of
the words of the chorus. It is as if the songwriter exclaimed
in awe as he was overcome by the unconditional love of God.
"O, the overwhelming, never-ending, reckless love of God…."
He must have been stunned by this self-giving love of God
and how intentional He is in pursuing lost and broken people
like us. More than just understanding this nature of God, I am
also a recipient of His "reckless" love. A little bit of research
revealed Cory Asbury's story behind the writing of this song.

Cory struggled to reconcile the image of a kind, tender, and
good God with his negative personal experience of who a
father was. In the latter part of his life, he asked God to show
him who He really is. Upon the birth of his first son, Gabriel,
Cory remembers thinking "…man, there's nothing this little
boy could ever do to make me love him any less." Cory goes
on to say, "And it was through that experience that I began to
see the Father rightly. That's the way He looks at me. I don't
have to earn His love, I don't have to do something to deserve
His affection and His heart. He just simply adores me because
I'm His son and I'm made in His image. And that changed
everything for me."[89]

When it comes to the use of the sometimes controversial word
"reckless", Cory had this to say: "…in the latter part of my life

I wasn't really a great human. ...I wasn't living a godly life-style. In my heart, in a lot of ways, I was against God. ...It's in that place where we're going, 'I'm completely against you' that [God is] saying: 'I don't care. I'm coming after your heart and [I'm going to] show you what love looks like on a cross, arms wide open, bleeding in this place of vulnerability and pain.' And [God says] 'No, it doesn't matter what it takes. It doesn't matter the cost.' ...The word 'Reckless' does not refer to God Himself; the God we are serving is not reckless. However, it refers to the way God loves us. If you try to consider what He did on the cross, He is utterly not concerned with the conse-quences of His actions in regards to His safety, comfort, and well being."[90]

My point is the same. It is not that God is reckless in His nature, but rather reckless in His pursuit and love toward us who need to be saved, encouraged, built up, and included in His family. Glory to His awesome Name!

Ministry Through Words and Music

Right on the heels of the song "Reckless Love" is another favourite of mine: "This is Amazing Grace". At the time of my writing of this chapter, I was gladly interrupted because my wife and I were going to hear a live 120-voice choir in St. Catharines, Ontario that evening. We were there at the invitation of a dear friend of ours who just happened to be one of the choristers. Wow! What an awesome evening of great music, worship, and adoration to God it was! The contempo-rary Christmas musical celebration we enjoyed was entitled *This Is Our Joy* and was presented under the choir directorship of Stuart Reimer. The presentation thrilled the more than 600 attendees in the auditorium that night.

Of the sixteen songs rendered by the choir, I would say I was most ministered to when they sang "This is Amazing Grace". Again, if you are not familiar with this song, give yourself a treat by pulling it up on YouTube. Be prepared to be blessed. Reflect on the words of this song, and you will quickly realize that the song writers, Jeremy Riddle, Josh Farro and Phil Wickham, incorporate "...Truth after truth about the greatness of God.... There are Bible references throughout the song. It's an amazing story.... The fact that our Creator would walk on the earth and gave us grace we don't deserve, that is something so worthy of celebration."[91] The words found in the first two stanzas were specifically used by the Holy Spirit to minister to me during my time of restoration.

This Is Amazing Grace[92]

Who breaks the power of sin and darkness
Whose love is mighty and so much stronger
The King of Glory, the King above all kings

Who shakes the whole earth with holy thunder
And leaves us breathless in awe and wonder
The King of Glory, the King above all kings

This is amazing grace
This is unfailing love
That You would take my place
That You would bear my cross
You lay down Your life
That I would be set free
Oh, Jesus, I sing for
All that You've done for me

Who brings our chaos back into order
Who makes the orphan a son and daughter

The King of Glory, the King of Glory
Who rules the nations with truth and justice
Shines like the sun in all of its brilliance
The King of Glory, the King above all kings

As I allowed the Holy Spirit to minister to me, I zeroed in on these truths: It is God, and God alone, who breaks the power of sin and darkness. It is this Almighty God whose love is so mighty and strong that I worship Him as the King above all kings. It is this God who keeps lavishing His amazing grace and unfailing love on me, even though I have grieved Him. It is this God who hung on the cross and so became a substitute for my sin. Through this gracious act I was set free from my sin and shame. It is this God I have resolved to love and serve for the rest of my days. For this and so much more, I want to sing about all He has done for me. Glory to His holy name!

FOR REFLECTION AND INTROSPECTION

1. Have you ever thought of God's love as being recklessly lavished upon you? And if so, does that change how you reciprocate your love for Him?

2. What favourite song of yours epitomizes how you feel about God and/or what he has done for you?

3. When you reflect on God's love for you, what thoughts are conjured up in your heart?

Chapter 7

DISCOVERING ME

"For I know that good itself does not dwell in me,
that is, in my sinful nature. For I have the desire
to do what is good, but I cannot carry it out."

Romans 7:18 NIV

ONE OF THE major reasons why we fall into the snare of deadly
sins is simply because we *do not* really know ourselves. I thought
I knew myself—but as it turned out, I was a little naïve and was
deceiving myself in making this claim. Discovering who you
truly are is important as it equips you to be a better Christian,
person, and leader. It helps you identify your strengths, discover your weaknesses, and uncover hidden blind spots in your
personality; blind spots that can cause you to stumble and fall.

However, one of the challenges of gaining a better understanding of ourselves is the fact that we have to delve into our
past; and more significantly, our painful past. "The past defines
nearly everything about us: our emotions, beliefs, desires, and
preferences. We are the sum of our history. To ignore it is to be
blind to the currents that sweep us along through life."[93] What
is even more interesting is why so many of us resist looking

back. First, we "want to believe that our present conflict is the issue." So if we can just fix the present conflict, we can continue on with our lives. Secondly, "all we want is to get rid of the pain." Consequently, we look for a quick fix and hope the pain will go away. But to dig up more pain to pile on top of what we are already feeling is the last thing we want to do.[94]

The fallout of my moral failure propelled me to take a fresh look into my past to rediscover who I really am, the lies I have believed about myself, and who I have become. But most important of all, I needed to rediscover who God wants me to be and how He wants to mould me to be more like Him.

So, what does self-discovery look like? How does one go about discovering who he really is?

There are several tools available to help us identify our unique personalities and the idiosyncrasies that come with each one. What follows here are a number of "tried and true" personality profile models that have served us well over the years. My hope is that from the three models I discuss you will be able to identify with at least one of them—and in so doing, be motivated to make the necessary changes to aid you in overcoming the weaknesses of your unique personality style.

During my period of restoration, I took personality tests I had done previously and participated in some new ones I came across in my readings. I undertook this exercise with the aim of discovering what my unique personality traits are in order to gain a better understanding of my character, temperament, and my sin bent. The first test I revisited was the Four Temperaments Profile. This helped me to refresh my understanding of my leadership style.

The Four Temperaments

The Four Temperaments is one of the more popular personality profiles. It has been in use for many years and has been proven to be very effective. The origin behind this profile traces back to the Ancient Greek medical theory of Humourism, which posits that an excess or deficiency of any of four distinct bodily fluids directly influences a person's health. These fluids, also known as humours, are black bile, yellow bile, blood, and phlegm.[95]

Greek physician Aelius Galen (Galenus in Latin) took this theory further and was of the view that the four humours not only affected health, but mood and personality as well. He went on to coin four terms to describe the four distinct personality types: melancholic (black bile), choleric (yellow bile), sanguine (blood), and phlegmatic (phlegm). Individuals with melancholic temperaments are creative, kind, and considerate; choleric people have energy, passion, and charisma; sanguine temperaments are extroverted and social; and phlegmatic temperaments are characterized by dependability, kindness, and affection.[96]

Let's take a closer look at each temperament.

The Melancholic Personality Type

These are your thinkers. They are genius-prone, very talented, and creative. Consequently, among this group you will find artists, musicians, and mathematicians. Their positive traits include being serious, purposeful, conscientious, idealistic, poetic, and philosophical. The Melancholic naturally wants to do things right and is quality oriented. These folks are highly perfectionistic and tend to place unrealistic expectations on themselves and others.

Melancholics are detailed oriented, operate from a plan, and are very private. They are introverted, logical, analytical, and factual in communication. They influence their environment by adhering to the existing rules and by doing things right according to predetermined standards. They are reserved and suspicious until they are sure of your intentions. However, they need to realize that not all people are like them and therefore should accept others for who they are. Striving for perfection is not wrong, but there are times when Melancholics expect too much from others because of their "perfectionist" attitude.[97]

Melancholics are moody. There are times when they feel happy, but then after a couple of minutes, they feel depressed or sad. They tend to remember the negative in any situation. They will get bogged down with details and can be hard to please. Nonetheless, they are schedule oriented, have high standards, and keep things organized. They are economical, tidy, neat, detail conscious, and able to identify creative solutions with ease.[98]

They are visionaries. They don't necessarily like teamwork because they don't trust anyone but themselves. They fear taking risks, making wrong decisions, and being viewed as incompetent. It is therefore no surprise that some of the things they consider unacceptable are: incompetence (this drives them up a wall!), disorganization (they must have a list), dishonesty, inaccuracy, blind faith, false impressions, wastefulness in any shape or form, and inconsistency.[99]

Other negative traits of Melancholics are that they tend to be loners and antisocial, but nonetheless they treat others with respect. They are sceptical, remote, and withdrawn and don't like to be opposed. They are not people oriented, and they hesitate to begin new projects.[100] But overall, they are very interesting people to be around.

The Choleric Personality Type

These are born leaders and very ambitious. They have a lot of aggression, energy, and passion and try to instil the same in others. They are very independent, inflexible, bossy, and impatient. They enjoy controversy and can debate anything. They are innovative, smart, specific, and direct and can overcome obstacles with ease. These folks will rise to any challenge you place before them.[101] They are multi-taskers and task-oriented people who are focused on getting the job done efficiently. They work well with heavy workloads. Cholerics are visionaries who seem to never run out of ideas, plans, and goals, which are all usually practical.

Cholerics are domineering, decisive, and opinionated, and they find it easy to make decisions for themselves as well as for others. They can dominate people of other temperaments (especially phlegmatic types) with their strong wills and can become dictatorial or tyrannical. They can be crusaders against social injustice, and they love to fight for a cause.

They don't like indecisiveness, weakness, and laziness. They like to be in charge of everything and are good at planning, as they often can immediately see a practical solution to a problem. However, they can quickly fall into deep depression or moodiness when failures or setbacks befall them. Cholerics do not easily empathize with the feelings of others or show compassion.

It is also worthwhile to be aware of this dynamic: The Choleric temperament has three combinations: Choleric-Sanguine, Choleric-Phlegmatic, and Choleric-Melancholy. "The traits of the *primary* temperament, Choleric, may be altered or modified in some significant way because of the influence of the *secondary* temperaments.[102]

The Sanguine Personality Type

Sanguines are naturally people-oriented. Their temperament is fundamentally impulsive and pleasure seeking, and they are very affectionate. As long as everybody is having a good time, the Sanguines are good. They are boisterous and tend to enjoy social gatherings and making new friends. They like popularity and are sociable and charismatic. They are extroverts, eternal optimists, talkers, very expressive, and influential. They are by far the most versatile of the four temperaments.

Because of their warm and appealing personality, people are automatically drawn to them. When they speak, they are very emotional and demonstrative, often using their hands and facial expressions. They are great storytellers and can engage you for hours just talking. They are great communicators who have the ability to influence people. It is no surprise then, that they are excellent motivational speakers. They are wordsmiths, very good on stage, and able to paint a picture well.[103]

Sanguine personalities generally struggle with following a task all the way through. They are also chronically late and tend to be forgetful and sometimes a little sarcastic. Often, when they pursue a new hobby, they lose interest as soon as it ceases to be engaging or fun. They are very much people persons. They prefer to talk a lot and tend to forget their obligations. Their confidence disappears instantly, and their decisions are based primarily on feelings. The only time Sanguines are silent is when they are asleep! They are great, fun-loving people and always full of bright ideas—but the real problem is that they don't follow through. They enjoy dressing according to current fashions.

Being undisciplined, unproductive, and egocentric are traits they need to improve upon. They tend to exaggerate and don't like details. They have a restless energy and can't sit still.

Sanguines need to do their best to avoid distractions. They need to appreciate their inner self and realize that there is more to life than just pure fun and humour. They need to recognize that everything we do should have meaning.[104]

Some of the things that Sanguines don't like include slowness and pessimism. They dislike solitude. They don't like to be bogged down in details and paperwork. In short, they don't like time restraints, a lot of structure, and when people show a lack of enthusiasm.

The Phlegmatic Personality Type

Phlegmatics are easy-going people. These relaxed and quiet people are by far the easiest of the four personalities with whom to get along—as long as you do not try to alter their routine or ask them to change. These are very dependable people, objective, diplomatic, and organized. They can be relied upon to be steady and faithful friends. They are accepting and affectionate, making friends easily. They are very practical people who will only do what must be done. They are highly intellectual, and consequently, enjoy studying, reading, and knowing about things.[105]

Phlegmatics make good parents. They tend to give their children enough time to do whatever they have to do and are not hurried like others. They are not easily upset. However, since they are usually easy going and tend to be lax with children, their home can become disorganized.

People with this kind of personality are steady and competent in the workplace. Their co-workers find them agreeable and peaceful. They also have the capability of managing administrative positions in a stress-free manner. Even when there is pressure at work, they can still perform duties and responsibilities well. They make good team players. They communicate a warm, sincere interest in others, preferring to have just a few friends. Because of their pleasant, enjoyable, and inoffensive personality, they make a lot of friends in a short time. They almost never become angry. They try to get along with everyone. They are incredibly controlled. They are good listeners, concerned, and compassionate and have a sense of humour, all of which explains why they have a wide circle of friends.[106]

Among the traits they need to work at, Phlegmatics are very unmotivated, selfish, and egotistical. They can be very self-protective and fearful as they don't want to be hurt. This also makes them indecisive. They tend to worry and have anxiety problems.

Phlegmatics tend to be good diplomats because their affable and non-judgmental nature makes reconciling differing groups easy for them. Phlegmatics prefer to observe and think about the world around them while not getting involved. They will conceal their true feelings; that is why they rarely get into fights. They prefer to walk away. While they make good friends, you will have to call them. They are the most introverted of the four personality types, but they will be there for you. It is interesting to know that they tend to be masculine and make up only 15 to 20% of the population.[107]

The Phlegmatic personality displays the gifts of mercy and love. They will give more of themselves when called upon, as opposed to giving money.

What Now?

So we have learned a little about these four temperaments/personality types; now what do we do with this information? First of all, after reading about each personality, you most likely want to find out which type you are—although chances are you may have already guessed just by reading the related traits. Discovering your personality can be easily achieved by doing a simple psychological on-line test that will take you less than five minutes. Tobias Cornwall, for example, has put together what he calls the Four Temperament test. This, he claims, will help you "find your most likely temperament blend." The results won't definitively say what your temperament is, although the more times you take the test, the more likely you are to end up with an accurate result.[108]

Psychologia has also put together a similar personality test for you to determine which of the four temperaments you are.[109] There are several other similar tests, so you may want to take two or three different tests, just to confirm your temperament type.

Once you have analyzed yourself and discovered what your primary personality trait is, you may wish to figure out what your spouse's and/or children's personalities are. Also, if this test has never been done at your place of employment, you may want to share it with your teammates to find out what personality types you are working with. This can end up being a very productive exercise and one that finally answers your questions as to why a certain co-worker acts the way he/she does.

By the way, don't be surprised if you see your traits in another personality type. That would be your secondary personality type. We all possess portions of all four types to varying degrees, but there tends to be one that is dominant and possibly one that is a secondary type. This is because while we are born with a specific personality trait, we may develop parts of others as we grow, interact with people, and learn new tasks.

With a knowledge of the characteristics of each personality type, you will notice certain dynamics as you interact with others. For example, Melancholic traits are opposite to Sanguine traits. Cholerics are the opposite of Phlegmatics. As you can imagine, conflicts are more likely to arise when individuals of opposing personality traits interact with one another. The key is to be aware, accommodating, and respectful of each other's temperaments and to take deliberate steps to mitigate potential areas of conflict.

I suspect you might have been wondering which one of the four temperaments fits my personality. Guess no more. I am Phlegmatic through and through. By studying my profile once again, I was able to easily connect personality traits—such as being affectionate, warm, interested in others, compassionate, and a good listener—with my propensity to cross the moral line. My love and genuine desire to see others live out the best version of themselves made me very vulnerable to hurting females. It is for reasons such as these that I want to stress the importance of knowing ourselves and our weaknesses and being very intentional about avoiding areas of our make-up that can ensnare us.

When we educate ourselves about the four temperaments and identify our personal strengths and weaknesses, we are, in essence, equipping ourselves to become better persons and leaders. When we choose to intentionally work on our weaknesses, we strengthen our character and resolve to be people of integrity. This has been my experience, and I trust this exercise will be as helpful to you as it has been to me.

Next, I took a look at my love style. I found this profile especially intriguing, and it led me to better understand how knowing our love styles can help us to be better leaders.

Profile of Your Love Styles

Another way to distinguish personality types is to identify your unique "love style" or "love imprint". In their book entitled *How We Love*, the Yerkovichs describe love styles/imprints as follows: "Each person's childhood experiences form the roots of who they are; continuing to inform the way that person responds to others or expresses love, even far into adulthood."[110] There are five love styles: The Avoider, The Pleaser, The Vacillator, The Controller, and The Victim.[111]

You may be tempted to ask, how is knowing my love style relevant to my leadership? It is important because it helps you to uncover who you are and how you relate to others—and in my case, especially how I relate to my wife. Like me, you will discover that your childhood experiences, over which you had no control, help to form part of the reasons why some people experience moral failures. Unfortunately, I can attest to this fact.

The Avoider Love Style

This is my love imprint. I identify as an Avoider. Avoiders, I have learned, are people who like to make decisions on their own. We can quickly assess a situation, come to a conclusion, and resolve the problem without ever feeling the need to consult anyone. Despite having worked as a team leader surrounded by great leaders, there are many times when I really don't see the need to involve others in my decision-making process. For me it feels like I am wasting their precious time, especially after I have already arrived at what I consider to be the best solution. I make decisions alone because I am not really open to other people's perspective on the decision in question when I feel that I have spent sufficient time brainstorming the issue. And most telling of all, seeking input from others sometimes conflicts with the way I am wired to take care of things independently.

In the past, I perceived this type of decision-making "skill" as a strength. But I have since learned that shutting out the contributions of others can come across as belittling, disengaging, or even emotionally distant. My wife experiences first-hand some of the flaws of my personality type and understandably does not hesitate to show her frustrations. She would say that living with me sometimes makes her feel as if she is not an equal partner in our marriage because I inadvertently exclude her from my decision-making processes. Looking back, I recognize that this trait was formed in my childhood, when "disconnecting" became my default response whenever I experienced a lack of comfort or nurturing. However, I have come to find out that this default response does not work well in marriage.

Then there is the quality that I wish I was able to reverse—that is, my inability to shed tears. While I see the value and appropriateness of tears, unfortunately this therapeutic form of release is not something that is easily accessible to me. For those who do not know me, I can at times be misconstrued as being an unemotional person. For example, when I have performed funeral services, I may have been perceived as uncaring or as someone merely going through the motions of my pastoral duties. However, those who know me well, know that nothing could be further from the truth.

The absence of my tears does not mean that I am detached from the emotional situation I may be facing. This is more accurately a learned behaviour that came out of my childhood experience of being humiliated in a classroom setting. It taught me to externally suppress my emotions and keep tears at bay whenever I experience grief.

When an Avoider like myself is assessed, he will admit to statements such as the following:

- I would describe myself as an independent, self-reliant person.

- When something bad happens, I get over it and move on.

- I like to make decisions on my own.

- Nothing gets me too bothered or upset.

- Events, remarks, and interactions with people who are upsetting to my spouse seem like no big deal to me. I believe in allowing people to be themselves.

- I rarely cry.

What all of these characteristics mean is simply this: The negative parts of my love imprint need to be acknowledged and put into their proper perspective by my spouse and other family members close to me. On the flip side of this coin, I also need to work harder at the undesirable aspects of my imprint so that they do not drive me into places of moral compromise. This is the main reason why I highly recommend that leaders be cognizant of their love imprint. Knowing this will do at least three things for you: 1.) Give meaning to some of your qualities and idiosyncrasies that you might have wondered about; 2.) Potentially cause you to work at being a better spouse, leader, and Christian; and 3.) Cause you to realize that this love imprint was made on your life at a very tender age when you had very little control over determining who you would like to become.

This is who I am. An Avoider. I believe you owe it to yourself to discover what your love imprint is and to take the necessary steps to better yourself. Doing so can make a world of difference to the way you do life as a person, but more so as a leader.

The third and final personality test that I would like to share with you comes from the work and research done by McIntosh and Rima in their classic book entitled, *Overcoming the Dark Side of Leadership*.

The Dark Side of Leaders

In laying the foundation for discussing this topic, the authors of *Overcoming the Dark Side of Leadership*, Gary L. McIntosh and Samuel D. Rima, have claimed that in order to overcome our dark side, we need first to understand it, then discover it, and finally redeem it. These topics, of course, are more adequately dealt with in the book in three distinct sections. So what follows is only designed to whet your appetite to learn more about the brilliant, scholarly work they have done. My hope is that you will be motivated enough to delve further into this crucial area of leadership and read the entire book and/ or seek out other views of leaders on this important subject. I must confess that I have emerged from my journey of doing both things a much better person and leader.

The whole point of identifying our dark side is to help us avoid making unwise, unethical, or immoral choices that have the potential to harm us and those we lead and serve. What follows are brief synopses of the five leadership types the authors have identified, and the dark sides associated with each.

The Compulsive Leader

Succinctly described, these are leaders who need to maintain absolute control. They micromanage people. They tend to be perfectionists who engage in excessive criticism of others. These leaders are also very status conscious and go out of their way to impress their colleagues.[112] In the position of pastors and spiritual leaders, "they feel the need to be in complete control of their organization in every minute detail."[113] This is sometimes disguised under the banner of pursuit of excellence in ministry. They also have the tendency to be excessively critical of issues.

The Narcissistic Leader

Image is everything for these leaders. For them, the world revolves on the axis of self. Consequently, they have an over-inflated sense of their importance to the organization and constantly seek the attention and admiration of others. They "overestimate their achievements and abilities, while stubbornly refusing to recognize the quality and value of the same in others."[114] The recognition of someone else's accomplishments poses a threat to their own self-importance. These traits are even more deadly among pastors. "Numerous churches have been destroyed by leaders who led the church into projects too energetic and costly for the congregation because the leader needed to feel good about himself."[115] Their bottom line is this: they are driven to succeed by a need for admiration and acclaim, not necessarily for the good of those they are called to serve.

The Paranoid Leader

Words that accurately describe these leaders are: suspicious, hostile, fearful, and jealous. These leaders are "desperately afraid of anything and anyone, whether real or imagined, they perceive to have even the remotest potential of undermining their leadership and stealing away the limelight."[116] Because of their suspicions of others, they will often create rigid structures and systems of control to ensure that they keep their finger in every piece of the organizational pie. As church leaders, they will never allow their board to meet without them being present. Excessive staff meetings and reporting are used to keep a tight rein on those around them. As senior pastors, they will not allow an associate to preach for fear the congregation might like the associate's preaching better than theirs.[117]

The Co-dependent Leader

These leaders are best known for pleasing others. This desire to please others causes them to take on additional tasks, even to the point where they overextend themselves. This is because saying no might hurt someone's feelings. They find it very hard to disappoint anyone.[118] As pastors, they find themselves being overtaken by the urgent needs of others while giving little attention to the overall direction of the church. Because this style of leadership fits my personality type, I will share a little more about this later.

The Passive-Aggressive Leader

Common traits found among these leaders include stubbornness, forgetfulness, and intentional inefficiency.[119] For a biblical model of the classic qualities of a passive-aggressive leader, McIntosh and Rima point us to Jonah. "Like this reluctant prophet, these leaders have a tendency to resist demands to adequately perform tasks. Their resistance is most often expressed through behaviours such as procrastination, dawdling, stubbornness, forgetfulness, and intentional inefficiency."[120]

These leaders are also prone to short outbursts expressing intense emotions, such as sadness, anger, and frustration. They tend to be "perennial complainers whose very presence demoralizes those whom they lead or with whom they interact." It is not uncommon to see them "exhibit impatience, irritability, and fidgeting when things are not going their way, or when they become bored with the proceedings."[121]

Why is it important to know our leadership strengths and weaknesses? It is simply because they serve as check points/reminders to us of our limitations, especially when we are dealing with difficult situations. Learning about the various qualities of these five types of leaders has also greatly assisted me to understand and identify the leadership blind spots of those who serve with me.

But before I delve in depth into my leadership style and outline the valuable lessons learned from my dark side, let me balance all this by talking about some of the more positive characteristics of leadership that we all need to strive to emulate. For this we turn our discussion to none other than the leadership style of Jesus.

It is good to know that regardless of what style epitomizes our leadership practice, we can all learn and be intentional in taking a positive model from Jesus.

C. Gene Wilkes in his classic book *Jesus on Leadership* gives us a healthy blueprint to consider.[122] If there is one thought that succinctly captures the leadership style of Jesus it might be this: He taught and embodied leadership as a service, not as a CEO or as someone who was blessed with special leadership skills. Jesus led from a service-oriented perspective. His, we can say, was the ministry of "the basin and the towel". From His humble ministry practices, we are made aware of a number of priceless leadership principles that epitome effective leaders.

These principles deal with issues such as the need for us to deflate our egos and practice instead a humbleness of heart. In this way, we can honestly cultivate a desire to be a follower of Christ. We are called to exemplify the meek nature of finding greatness in serving God and majoring in what I call the ministry of the "towel and the basin."

In his principles, Wilkes also encourages us to take risks while sharing responsibilities and authority. For these are all a part of building a great team of servant leaders that exemplify Christ. Someone once accurately described TEAM as Together Each Achieves More. The operative word here, I believe, is *together*, not just the boss doing all the heavy lifting.

My Leadership Style

Now going back to the analysis of the Co-dependent Leader, I will admit that this leadership style accurately describes me. This revelation clarified for me why I led the way I did, valued the people I served, and ultimately made it easier to cross the moral line the way I did. I am now a firm believer that each leader needs to be honest with himself/herself and find out the negative and positive traits that accompany his/her leadership style.

I was reminded that co-dependency is "an emotional, psychological, and behavioural condition that develops as a result of an individual's prolonged exposure to, and practice of, a set of oppressive rules—rules that prevent the open expression of feeling as well as the direct discussion of personal and interpersonal problems."[123]

Some of the problematic characteristics McIntosh and Rima share about co-dependent leaders unfortunately have been lived out in my leadership. For example, I find myself at times taking personal responsibility for the actions and emotions of others, and sometimes even graciously attempting to deal with the inappropriate behaviour of others. I find myself going to the extreme to avoid hurting a person's feelings. I try to avoid confrontation at all costs and would prefer to serve as a peacemaker between hostile parties. Consequently, people with my leadership personality find it very difficult whenever they have to confront and deal with unacceptable behaviour by adults, especially in the church.[124] As you might have already detected, our personality type does not serve us well, especially when dealing with conflicts or problem solving.

It is easy to see why certain personality types can become attracted to pastoral leadership positions. I found that my propensity to feel I need to "fix" people's problems gave me a sense of being God's hands extended. However, I also discovered that in counselling with members of the opposite sex, a situation may arise in which I move from being a "fixer" to unintentionally setting myself up for moral compromise. In doing so, I become prone to allowing a person's urgent need to become a priority of mine. Leaders like myself therefore need to accept the fact that we are not responsible for the attitudes and actions of others. Rather, pleasing God is more important than being liked by the people we serve.

Lessons Learned About Our Dark Side

So what lessons can we learn about our dark sides of leadership? As has become obvious, there are some valuable lessons we can all learn from the different leadership qualities we possess. Hopefully, among other benefits, they can help to serve as safeguards to keep us on the straight and narrow path. They also serve to remind us that the position of trust we hold does not give us licence to abuse its power by rewarding ourselves in ways that are sinful and displeasing to God. Instead, we need to embrace the fact that our true identity and fulfillment is still found in none other than Jesus Christ. We need to remember that we are first accountable to God for our behaviour and then to those He permits us to serve. All attempts to reward ourselves for the good work we think we have accomplished only leads to sin and degradation.

Another point that is worthy of acknowledgment is the fact that we need to carefully examine our negative past to see what adjustments can be made that will have a positive impact on our future. My journey back to wholeness in God has revealed some alarming discoveries that align with the reason for my fall.

For example, I found it quite interesting to see how my counsellor connected my traumatic childhood classroom experience with my inappropriate adult behaviour. What a revelation and freeing experience that was for me! As shared earlier in chapter one, that embarrassing and humiliating childhood experience I suffered left an indelible mark on my life. Among other things, it revealed that when I am faced with a difficult, threatening situation, my tendency is to find a safe place to reboot my self-esteem. And that place is not always good. Of course, while we cannot change our childhood experiences, we can learn from them and consequently avoid the negative influences they have the power to impose on us.

One of the main reasons why we revisit our past is to gain freedom from the power that our dark side can wield against us. One practical and biblical way of doing this would include such steps as asking for forgiveness from people we have offended. Whether it is a face-to-face meeting with an individual, or reading a letter of confession from a pulpit to those affected by our behaviour, we must ask for forgiveness.

Fast Forward to Today

Whenever I bump into people I have not seen since my public confession, I ask them to forgive me for the way my behaviour hurt them. Most respond graciously by telling me that they, and God, have already forgiven me and therefore all is well. In my response, I thank them and affirm that truth, but quickly go on to share that I violated the trust they had placed in me, and I am deeply sorry about that. I do this to show them we should not confuse forgiveness with trust. The former is much easier to receive than the latter. Trust, on the other hand, needs to be rebuilt.

While all this sounds humble and modest, balance is required. We need to be careful that we are not unduly hard on ourselves for the sins and failures of our past. We know all too well that these have the power to haunt and cripple us from moving on with our lives and ministries. Scripture reminds us of why forgiveness is necessary: "…in order that Satan might not outwit us. For we are not unaware of his schemes." (2 Corinthians 2:11 NIV). A lack of forgiveness is a major tool the enemy uses to gain entrance into a believer's life and then keep him in bondage. We therefore need to be careful not to give the enemy a foothold. We can avoid this by leaving our unresolved conflicts and past anger at the foot of the cross. As someone accurately said, the greatest definition of forgiveness is letting another person off the hook so that we can go free. Amen!

Discovering Ourselves and Our Limits

A major part of discovering ourselves lies in our ability to admit our limitations and capabilities.

As pastors of large congregations, we find ourselves facing unrealistic expectations and subtle pressures from our Deacon Boards. With their encouragement, we develop job descriptions that are so onerous that they would require at least two individuals to perform all the duties. Added to this are also the subtle pressures that come from our congregations. In an article written by Garrett Kell, he cites this statistic: "On average, churchgoers expect their pastor to juggle sixteen major tasks each week!"[125] Such expectations are both unrealistic and overwhelming.

Good leadership training cautions us to resist these kinds of pressures. But on the positive side, expectations can also serve as a motivation to help us achieve our God-given goals, provided we are honest enough to tailor them to our capabilities. There is wisdom in letting our superiors know how we feel about what is expected of us, and we should avert setting ourselves up for burnout.

Boards are sometimes notorious for placing unrealistic expectations on their lead pastors, while at the same time failing to provide adequate protection for us. In response, the lead pastors also give impractical job descriptions to their team members. This of course perpetuates unnecessary stress. While high expectations should be required of our leaders, subtle pressures do not make for a healthy and happy work environment. As a result, we spread ourselves so thinly that we become ineffective in meeting the more spiritual needs of our congregations.

Faced with circumstances like these, lead pastors are lured into moving from a forty to fifty-hour workweek to a sixty to seventy-hour week. We excuse ourselves from this ungodly practice with the super spiritual thought that we are just fulfilling the "call" placed on our lives. But are we? While fulfilling expectations and doing long hours are sometimes necessary, they must be placed in the proper context of what God requires of us. After all, it is His church we are assisting in building, not ours. We should not neglect other aspects of our lives, like spending quality time with family and loved ones.

Again, we understand that expectations are a wholesome way of being held accountable to those in authority over us. However, from a human perspective, expectations can either propel people to achieve or can produce pain and failure. Sometimes the weight of expectations can cause even the most compliant and well-intentioned leader to snap under the heavy load. Under its influence, many pastors have found themselves turning to self-destructive and sinful behaviours as a way of escaping the pressure of the outcome they have failed to produce. These "escapes" can range from consuming alcoholic beverages, gambling, pornography, adultery, and everything in between. All of these produce a recipe for burnout and/or moral failure.

There have been times when the demands of ministry forced me to read and study the Word merely for sermon preparation. I'm embarrassed to admit this. But I suspect that I'm not alone in this ungodly practice. Setting time aside to simply connect with God and hear what He may be saying to me became less and less of a discipline as other aspects of ministry required more of my time. A word of caution is appropriate here for my friends who can identify with these realities. There is no substitute for spending time in the Word, in prayer, and allowing the Holy Spirit to speak to us as we conduct the business of the church. Ignoring this fact is a clear sign that our leadership engine is running on empty.

One of the disciplines I had built in to my ministry requirements was to schedule a personal two-day retreat each month. These were done away from the office at a quiet retreat centre. But on more occasions than I care to admit, these two days were turned into "catch up on administrative work and leadership issues" days. So the real soul-searching questions and reflections that should have been addressed on these retreats were not done. Questions such as: "Where have I gotten sloppy in my Christian disciplines? What have I been neglecting? How is my personal relationship with God? How well have I been managing my time? What does God want to say to me about my leadership to His people? Unfortunately, because of my regular heavy workload, questions like these were rarely addressed. These retreats were supposed to model Jesus' practice of resorting to a quiet place to pray, but unfortunately, more often than not, this desired outcome was not accomplished. If as a pastor/leader you can identify with my dilemma, you would be wise to learn from my mistakes and set better priorities. Know your limits and work within them.

The Value of Discovering One's Self

We have seen that wisdom requires that we become intentional in knowing who we are. Leaders who are oblivious of their blind spots, dark sides, and the revelations from their personality profiles will inadvertently end up shipwrecking their ministry.

In 2015, Howard Hendricks conducted a study entitled *The Pattern Among Fallen Pastors.*[126] In it, he examined 246 men in full-time ministry who had experienced moral failure within a two-year period. As far as Hendricks could discern, these full-time clergy were all born-again followers of Jesus. Though they shared a common salvation, these men also shared a common feat of devastation: They had all been involved in an adulterous relationship over a 24-month period.[127]

After interviewing each man, Hendricks compiled four common characteristics of their lives:

1. None of the men was involved in any kind of real personal accountability.

2. Each of the men had all but ceased having a daily time of personal prayer, Bible reading, and worship.

3. More than 80 percent of the men became sexually involved with the other woman after spending significant time with her, often in counselling situations.

4. Without exception, each of the 246 men had been convinced that sort of fall would never happen to them.[128]

In the findings of this simple study, we are once again given an inside look into some of the vulnerable areas of our lives in which Satan works at monopolizing. What is interesting about these statistics is the fact that as go pastors, so go other white-collar workers, tradespeople, housewives, and anyone who has ceased to nurture their daily personal walk with God. I don't believe that any of them had set out to shipwreck their ministry. But like them, when we are ignorant of the devil's vices, coupled with not knowing our weaknesses and propensity to sin, we run the risk of ending up as a negative moral statistic—or at the very minimum, we set ourselves up to be in bondage to sin. The Apostle James reminds us of this truth: "Anyone, then, who knows the good he ought to do and doesn't do it, sins." (James 4:17 NIV).

We therefore need to do the hard work of defining who we are, refining our personality, and determining that we will choose straight paths for ourselves. It was Friedrich Nietzsche who once brilliantly noted, "He whose life has a why can bear almost any how."[129] What is your why? And how well do you know yourself?

FOR REFLECTION AND INTROSPECTION

1. Do you know who you really are? Or the way others perceive you? If not, I recommend that you take one or two personality tests to discover who you are.

2. Which personality type describes you best? Do you see a connection between your type and the way you lead and are received?

3. Have you been able to identify your love and leadership style? Knowing your love and leadership style also speaks volumes about who you are and the positive and negative ways you lead and navigate life.

Chapter 8

RENOVATING THE HEART

"The heart is the most deceitful of all things, and desperately wicked. Who really knows how bad it is?"

Jeremiah 17:9 NLT

I LIKE WORKING with wood—making furniture and fixing wooden articles that are broken. A few years ago, when my granddaughter was seven years old, she conferred upon me an unmerited reputation that I have since been trying to live up to. To this day she emphatically claims that: "Granddad can fix anything!" *I am* fearful about what her response will be when she finally realizes that I am unable to live up to her impression.

I have also done a fair bit of home renovations in my time, and especially gotten saddled with gutting and rebuilding washrooms from scratch. As all builders know, a renovation project is never complete without some unwanted surprise—one that extends the project and adds to the original estimated timeline and cost of the job. But such is the nature of renovations.

But homes are not the only things that need renovations. Did you know that our hearts are in need of renovation too? And unlike homes, heart renovation is internal work. "If the heart is not changed, then all recovery from sexual addiction and all restoration is, at best, blissful ignorance that contradicts the teaching of Jesus."[130]

In his classic book, *Renovation of the Heart, Putting on the Character of Christ,*[131] Dallas Willard takes us through what I would describe as a major overhaul or transformation of the heart. His premise is as follows: Our hearts are a spiritual place within us; a place from which our outlook, choices, and actions come. Unfortunately, our hearts were formed by a world away from God, and as such, the greatest need we have as humans is the need to have our hearts renovated and changed to Christlikeness.[132] I concur. Many of the truths taught and expressed in this book have been used by the Holy Spirit to renovate my heart. Consequently, I would like to share some of Willard's thoughts with you. I hope you too can derive some benefit from them.

The sinful choices I made had a negative effect on my body and spirit. But even more revealing, they were done as a direct outworking of the condition of my heart. Understand then, that when the prophet Jeremiah says, "The heart is more deceitful than all else, and is desperately sick," he is making an honest assessment of us. Or more personally, he is describing my heart. When we are at the place where we can scrupulously admit this, I believe the foundation is then laid for our spiritual formation or reformation into Christlikeness.

My Restoration Journey

In Ezekiel 36:26, God's promise to restore Israel was not only physical but also spiritual. To accomplish this, God would give the Israelites a new heart for following Him. Verse 26 captures this loving and gracious act of God. "And I will give you a new heart, and I will put a new spirit in you. I will take out your stony, stubborn heart and give you a tender, responsive heart." (NLT). This verse has both challenged and encouraged me at the same time. The challenge is to ensure that the new work the Holy Spirit is doing in my heart is not frustrated.

My journey of being restored to God began immediately after I made my confession to the congregation. Standing in the church's parking lot that Sunday afternoon, I suddenly realized that my ministry had just prematurely concluded. But God had already gone ahead of me and raised up men and women to aid in this new, uncertain journey upon which my wife and I were about to embark. My restoration journey was kick-started when a close, long-standing friend of ours said to me: "Pastor Colin, take this gift. I want you and Dorselie to get away from this environment for a little while." That significant sum of money was not only in keeping with the generous spirit of the individual, but I saw it as a signal that we needed to begin our restoration immediately.

A few days later, a dear colleague and friend of mine approached us with another gift. We were told that arrangements had been made for us to meet with a couple who did marriage counselling. The timing of this and the ministry we received turned out to be a huge blessing and healing for us. These counsellors were mightily used by God to help us begin the healing process. By the end of that weekend, renovations on my heart were well on the way.

I vividly recall a revelation I received during one of the counselling sessions that truly helped me to understand who I had become as an adult. For the first time in my life I was able to make the connection between a negative childhood experience

I had when I was around age ten and the way I handled conflict in my life. For me, this revelation was a God moment. I specifically felt the Holy Spirit ministering directly to me in that session. I am very grateful to have received this gift to attend a private counselling retreat, and I am thankful for the love and care shown to us by this friend of ours.

God continued to provide the resources we needed for this season of our lives. A group of friends got together at Christmas and threw a wonderful party for us as an expression of their love and appreciation for us. As you might anticipate, they also tangibly showed their love through giving us appropriate and thoughtful gifts. Thanks friends, and glory to the Most High God who still demonstrates His love to His people even when they mess up.

Towards the end of 2016, the restoration program that our fellowship arranged for us got started. Dorselie and I spent a few quality days in Akron, Ohio, at Emerge Counseling Services. Over these days, we received eight professional hours of counselling from one of their seasoned counsellors, Dr. Donald Lichi. During these counselling sessions, the Lord did a number of beautiful things for Dorselie and me. One quality of our counsellor that especially stood out was the love and care that exuded from him as he toggled between what he sensed the Holy Spirit was impressing upon him, and what he knew needed to be addressed in our lives. I loved the way he waited for direction from the Holy Spirit before proceeding to minister to us. It became obvious that both his skills and experience were being used by the Holy Spirit to accomplish a healing work in our lives.

I also deeply appreciated the fact that our counsellor was anything but judgmental, self-righteous, or condemnatory in all of his dealings with us. This humble spirit continued throughout all the sessions. Dorselie and I were blessed to see how he loved on us and showed genuine care and concern to see our hearts renewed. In short, he left an indelible godly impression on us.

After administering a battery of tests,[133] our counsellor was able to connect the dots in my life. From his vast experience with clients like myself, he was able to identify my temperament, weaknesses, and sensitivities—all of which clearly pointed to the reason why I could be at risk to experience a moral failure.

The ultimate goal of my counsellor in all of this was first to restore my relationship with God, and consequently, set me back on the right path of life. I felt safe and comfortable sharing my life's story with him. After spending hours with us, his conclusions were accurate, in keeping with who I am, and what I had done. Consequently, I felt I was empowered to work towards achieving the recommendations he had made for my personal and ministerial restoration.

Months after returning from Akron, Ohio, I read the book *Renovation of the Heart* by Dallas Willard. It was the perfect follow up to the counselling we had received. It stood out, in my mind, as one of the best books recommended to me to aid in my restoration. Willard underscores the importance of the heart. It is the central place from which we live, operate, and organize our lives. It is the place that houses our choices. And choice is where sin dwells. It therefore behoves us to honestly examine our hearts to discover the true condition and deficiencies that lie within. If the heart is misaligned with God's will, our lives and actions will naturally follow and be contrary to His will as well. As such, recognition of our heart's condition forms the first step in our spiritual formation/reformation in

Christ; a process that would culminate in a love for God with all of our hearts, souls, minds, and strength.

The book also gave me a fresh perspective on the power of temptation and sin. We are tempted when we think about sinning and marinate on those thoughts instead of immediately dismissing them. The moment we mentally say "yes" to the temptation, we commit sin at that point—even though we may not physically act it out. In Mathew 5:27-28, Jesus emphasized this truth: "You have heard that it was said, 'You shall not commit adultery.' But I tell you that anyone who looks at a woman lustfully has already committed adultery with her in his heart."

I was reminded of the fact that whatever my action is, it comes out of my whole person—which includes my thoughts, feelings, will, body, and soul. Our actions are an external representation of who we truly are on the inside. When we are living a life apart from God, the order of dominance looks like this: body, soul, mind (i.e. thought/feeling), spirit, and God last. In this case, the needs of the body drive the decisions and actions of the individual. In contrast, in a life submitted to God, the order of dominance looks like this: God, spirit, mind, soul, and then body. In this instance, God's power and influence permeates the whole person. Each part is surrendered to the will of God, and the person is able to live a God-fearing life.

From this we see that spiritual transformation is not something we can achieve on our own—no matter how hard we try. Rather, it is achieved as we intentionally and continuously yield our wills to God and allow His transformative power to touch and reform each aspect of our beings: spirit, mind, soul, and body. I found this to be so true. I can now attest to this fact from personal experience.

As a leader who crossed the moral line, I realized, albeit too late, that my failure was not just related to what I had done, but more importantly, to my heart's condition and hence my total being that was revealed by the act. I can now appreciate why David pleaded with God to create in him a clean heart and to renew a right spirit within him. (Psalm 51:10). Today I issue a similar plea to my readers: If the foregone description of the heart comes anywhere close to what you may be presently experiencing, I urge you to surrender your heart afresh to God. Allow Him to renew it as only He can. Determine now to get off the sin trail and allow the Holy Spirit to renovate your heart. He will, if you are serious in this goal.

Renewing Our Intimacy with God

Undoubtedly, getting back in a right relationship with God is the first and most important step in the renovation process. Sin begins in our thought life. As such, thoughts are the first place where change can, and must, begin to occur. Here, the Spirit of God transforms our minds and begins to direct our will to be in alignment with God's.

You may ask: Why is it so crucial that our thought life be transformed? It is simply because the realm of thought involves four main factors: ideas, images, information, and our ability to think.[134] Willard offered an in-depth analysis of this, but on this platform, I will focus on "ideas" and "images", as they are the most powerful factors. For the full teaching on this topic, I refer you to the sixth chapter of *Renovation of the Heart*.

Everyone has ideas—good, bad, and indifferent. Ideas are abstract and general assumptions of reality and cannot be precisely defined or specified. So it is not easy for us to pinpoint which ideas inform our decisions or govern our lives. We must therefore be alert and ensure we replace ungodly ideas with the truths that Jesus embodied and taught us—Kingdom of God ideas. This is what the Apostle Paul meant in Romans 12:2 when he admonished us to have our minds renewed.

Images that occupy our mind, on the other hand, "are always concrete or specific, as opposed to the abstractness of ideas, and are heavily laden with feeling. They frequently present themselves with the force of perception and have a powerful emotional and sensuous linkage to governing idea systems."[135] Hence images are worse. They are more seductive and have the power to dominate our thought life to the point where we begin to feel we must indulge. Images quickly become a primary stronghold of evil in us. They become Satan's efforts to defeat God's purposes for our lives. They have the power to obsess and to hypnotize, as well as to escape critical scrutiny.

So here is the solution to this problem: We have to replace those destructive images and ideas with the images and ideas that filled the mind of Jesus. The most obvious thing we can do to train our thought life to think godly thoughts is to draw from certain key portions of Scriptures. We each have our favourites. Let's make them a permanent fixture in our minds. Memorize them. Mediate on them. Use them in our prayers. Live by them. In essence, what we are doing is training or re-training our minds to replace darkness with the light of the Word. It works!

Take, for instance, Paul's counsel to us: "Whatever is true, whatever is honourable, whatever is right, whatever is pure, whatever is lovely, whatever is of good repute, if there is any excellence and if anything is worthy of praise, let your mind dwell on these things." (Philippians 4:8 NAS). Willard describes this verse as "a fundamental and indispensable part of our spiritual formation in Christ."[136] Dwelling on God's word assists us in the transformation of our thinking from sinful thoughts to Christlikeness. This discipline makes room for the Holy Spirit to work in us, and it permits destructive feelings to be perceived and dealt with for what they truly are—our will and not God's will. Other passages that would be helpful to meditate upon include: Joshua 1:8, Psalm 1, Romans 5:1-8 or 8:1-15, 1 Corinthians 13, and Colossians 3:1-17.

As powerful as ideas and images are, feelings pose an even greater threat to our living a life of obedience to God. We all have feelings—good and bad alike. They are sometimes so strong that we erroneously believe that they must be acted upon. With a few exceptions, feelings are good servants but disastrous masters. With respect to bad or destructive feelings, we are counselled to replace them with good ones or to subordinate them in a way that makes them constructive and transforms their effects. If not, we run the risk of having our feelings exercise total mastery over us. At all stages of our lives, feelings are among Satan's primary instrument used to devastate our soul. When you consider that most people base their decisions primarily on how they feel at that moment in time, you can understand why our world is prone to gross immoralities and addictions.

Sin's Problem and Solution

We sometimes tend to lightly dismiss sin as simply missing the mark God has set for us. But a deeper biblical understanding of sin reveals this sobering truth: Sin in reality is not wanting to be oneself before God. It is refusing to find our deepest identity in our relationship and service to God. It is the making of good things into ultimate things. It is an attempt to fill voids.

"It is seeking to establish a sense of self by making something else more central to your significance, purpose, and happiness than your relationship to God."[137] Sin's place of origin is in the heart. And this is why: "The solution to sin is not to impose an ever-stricter code of behaviour. It is to know God."[138]

Understand that "the essence of sin is not [primarily] the violation of laws but a wrecked relationship with God, one another, and the whole created order."[139]

It is therefore wise for us to adhere to the wisdom shared in Proverbs 4:23: "Guard your heart above all else, for it determines the course of your life." (NLT). This is not just true, but also wise, godly advice. It is given because the heart represents the centre of emotions, thinking, and reasoning. The heart plays a crucial role in the battle between wisdom and foolishness, between righteousness and evil.[140] So we watch over our hearts because our lives, that is, our words and behaviour, flow from our hearts. Every thought originates from the heart.

FOR REFLECTION AND INTROSPECTION

1. What slippery slopes do you gravitate toward during stressful times? In what ways can you set a guard over your heart?

2. What do you miss most when your intimacy with God is broken? What do you do to reconnect your heart with His?

3. Sin, in reality, is not wanting to be one's self before God. Do you agree with this statement?

Chapter 9

RESTORATION

"Restore to me the joy of your salvation,
and make me willing to obey you."

Psalm 51:12 NLT

THE VERY SOUND of the word *restoration* implies the hope of wholeness, a new beginning, a fresh start. But it first implies that a failure has occurred. The actual meaning of the word is, "the reinstating of a previous practice, right, or situation." It is the act of restoring something or someone to their original condition. "To be restored is to return to a place of obedience, blessing, and usefulness before God."[141]

As a credential holder with the Pentecostal Assemblies of Canada, I first acknowledged my guilt at having violated our biblically based shared values. I then requested and was accepted into a formal restoration program by the District Executive of my home district, Eastern Ontario and Nunavut, with The Pentecostal Assemblies of Canada. This provided me with specific accountability relationships in a personal supervisory program. I also had the privilege of receiving professional help through Emerge Counseling Services in Akron,

Ohio. Key recommendations from this were then enhanced by additional therapists back home through the ministry of Shalem Counselling Services—Clergy Care.

Over a period of three years, I was privileged to be surrounded by a number of great counsellors, colleagues, and friends. They all had one thing in common: They genuinely wanted to see me restored. Permit me to take a moment here to share of few of the deposits that these individuals have made into my life.

Case in point: At the beginning of my restoration journey, and right through to its conclusion, I had the good fortune of having one Rev. Frank Patrick as my official accountability pastor. As one of our highly respected senior officers and Church Health Care facilitator, he was assigned to me by our District. Frank lives up to his name. He is very forthright and honest, and has gained this reputation because he is a very nurturing and considerate leader in our fellowship. Added to these qualities, we are also friends.

Included in the deposits Frank made into my life are the countless articles that he sends, the sobering discussions we have engaged in, and the many hours we have met just for fellowship. Frankly speaking, he is a man who understands the times we live in and is flexible enough to continually make the necessary adjustments to his life and ministry in order to remain effective, current, and relevant to his calling. Thanks Frank.

A few months into my restoration program, while doing a Google search, I stumbled upon a book entitled *Restoring the Fallen*,[142] written by a team of authors. It turned out to be the additional kind of help I needed at that season of my life. One of the recommendations received through counselling was to establish an accountability team to walk with me through this season. After reading the book, I felt a clear impression from the Holy Spirit to approach a few of my friends/colleagues and request them to support me through that season of my life. They would form what is referred to as a Spiritual Care Team.

By way of definition, the authors of *Restoring the Fallen* described a Spiritual Care Team this way: "Sometimes a serious physical illness can land us in the hospital's intensive care unit (or ICU). A Spiritual Care Team is another kind of ICU. It is a group of mature Christians who voluntarily commit themselves to support and assist a person…with acute spiritual needs through a process of returning that person to fellowship with God, family, and fellow believers."[143]

Weeks later, four quality leaders were handpicked by the Holy Spirit to be a part of my Spiritual Care Team. I say the Holy Spirit "hand-picked" them because there were at least three other friends I had planned to approach, but by God's design they did not make the cut.

Among the things these men had in common, four qualities stood out: 1.) They are humble men who love the Lord; 2.) They are all married and have healthy marital and family relationships; 3.) They are all proven credible leaders and pastors in our community; and 4.) They love me and wanted to see me restored. They committed to meeting with me for one year, once a month, to pray with and care for me. The first person I felt led to approach was Sam Sibley.

Sam Sibley was chosen to give leadership to the team because of his genuine concern to find out what had gone wrong in my life and what he could do to assist me in my restoration process. He is the lead pastor of a growing church in our community and graciously assumed this responsibility amidst a very hectic pastoral schedule. I have developed a deep appreciation for him because of how honestly and authentically he deals with challenging situations. I love the fact that he does not seek to sugarcoat issues that need to be addressed directly. While being direct, he is also gracious. He is the real deal.

Derek Clarke gives leadership as Executive Director to a group of leaders who are a part of a successful wellness company. In the past, he has capably filled the role of a small group pastor in the church he attends, and in doing so, has led a number of married couples to wholeness in their relationships with each other. As a leader, Derek has experienced much success in both corporate and Christian leadership circles.

Jason Luscombe is an Assistant to the District Superintendent of Eastern Ontario and Nunavut Districts, in Ministry Services. The humility and sincerity of this man stand out as enviable qualities among his peers. The love, respect, and friendship he has shown to me served as healing virtues to my restoration. He epitomizes what servant leadership is all about. I will always remember and be grateful for the deposits he made into my life during our year-long meetings.

Anthony Nelson and his wife Cheryl are founders of Faith Five Fellowship of Ministries. His passion to restore, equip, train, and release leaders is very evident in what he does and the success he has experienced. Pertaining to sharing the good news of the gospel, Anthony sees no barriers or differences among denominations. His quest is to be God's hand extended in reaching his community for God. This has been his mission since 1993.

What a crew! Interacting with these men on a regular basis reminded me that we all need others who love us enough to confront us honestly and tell us when we're off-track or going in the wrong direction.

To say that I enjoyed those monthly meetings with these friends would not be an accurate assessment. I endured some of the meetings, felt very vulnerable in others, and experienced the weight of my behaviour in some, but I undoubtedly benefitted from all of them. There were sessions in which it would have been easier for me to withhold important information from this accountability team. But this was not an option. I was there to assist them to perform their task well. And that they did! I received the help I needed at that stage of my life, when it was most crucial.

During these meetings, amazing transformative work was done by the Holy Spirit. As you will judge from some of the questions below which Sam compiled for our monthly discussions, these sessions were intense, deep, and brutally honest. I experienced tough love, but it came with the strong resolve of my friends to see me nurtured back to spiritual health.

Using the book *Restoring the Fallen* as a guide, my friends encouraged me through the discussion of tough questions/topics. What follows is a compilation of some of these gruelling questions:

- What have you been learning about yourself during this season of your life? (This was a standard lead-in question that was asked every month at the beginning of each session.)

- How do you view women? What need/void do they fill in your life?

- What were the internal weaknesses that led to the affair?

- Where is the lapse in character and integrity, and how do we help to re-build that?

- What is the proof that you are willing to be restored? What is the evidence of repentance?

- What will it require of you to love Dorselie (that is my wife) even if she disrespects you?

- Have you confessed to Dorselie your old patterns that helped make the affair possible?

- Who haven't you talked to about this affair that you need to? In other words, is there anyone you are avoiding?

- How do you stay honestly content even if your sexual needs aren't being met?

- Going forward, what boundaries do you need to set in your relationship with females?

- How are you doing with your boundaries?

- What have you learned from the consequences of your actions?

- What things are you holding as secrets in your heart because they are too painful to admit?

- What lies did you have to tell Dorselie in order to keep the affair going?

- What are some areas that you find yourself struggling with or wishing that we wouldn't talk about?

- Have you had temptations in the past few months, and if so, how have you dealt with them?

- What does the future look like for you personally and for Dorselie?

Dorselie was invited to attend one of the sessions and the same care and love that was meted out to me was also lavished on her. During this first year of restoration, as one might expect, Dorselie's emotions were still very raw. At times, she reminded me that I was responsible for the way her life and ministry had been drastically altered. Nevertheless, she attended the session for the following reasons:

- She was glad I had reached out to a group of credible men who were caring enough to walk with me through this period of my life.

- She knew that these leaders had our best interests for restoration at heart. Consequently, their attitude would be gracious instead of being judgemental. This of course, turned out to be absolutely true.

- She saw this meeting as an opportunity to share aspects of her story and confirm that our relationship was once again moving in the right direction.

I am so thankful to Dorselie for co-operating with this plan and for demonstrating solid Christian virtues. Of course, in her quiet moments, there were times when she saw herself as a victim of a circumstance she had very little control over. This made her both mad and sad. There were times when I did not know whether or not the next phone call, visit, or the untimely meeting of someone would trigger her anger or disappointment in me. Looking back on that period, we chuckle over a comment a good friend of ours recommended to me as a response: "Just take your beatings." And that I did.

To spouses who have, or unfortunately may, find themselves in Dorselie's quandary, I recommend that you "hold the course". Look ahead and trust God for better days. While the hurt and embarrassment are real and seemingly never ending, leaving your spouse is not the wisest decision. Sure, the Bible makes provision for terminating your marriage in the case of adultery, but there is life and hope after an adulterous affair. There is, for example, room for growth and introspection and the opportunity to model what true forgiveness and commitment look like in marriage. For demonstrating all these Christian qualities, I have grown to deeply love, highly commend, and genuinely respect Dorselie.

Today, as I reflect on the healing sessions I had with my spiritual care team, I consider myself blessed and give God thanks for each of these gentlemen. The time, commitment, care, and love they gave towards seeing me restored is so much appreciated. For the many prayers, tough conversations, and godly counsel I received, I say a heart-felt thanks to my brothers. God bless you guys.

Restored to God

All sin separates and sometimes even severs us from an intimate relationship with God. Once we give in to temptation, we are never the same again. The need then arises to be reinstated to God. For a protracted period during this season apart from God, both my private and corporate worship experiences seemed empty and meaningless. I realized I had moved away from God, not vice versa. When I prayed, it felt like a one-way conversation. Not that God had chosen to be silent, but rather I became very cognizant of the grief that my sin had caused Him.

For those who have experienced this, or something similar, it appears as if we are separated from God by miles. Emptiness reigns in our heart. In short, it is an awful, debilitating feeling and one that Satan magnifies to the point where we begin to believe there is no way back to God. And so I share this awful season of my life to warn my fellow colleagues to stay clear from the sins of the flesh.

So how can we pull out of this spiritual slump? By returning to the same disciplines we instilled in our lives BEFORE we went astray. We need first of all to get back to protracted periods of reading, reflecting, and studying the Word of God. During these times of spiritual dryness, praying becomes a major struggle. Our thoughts are pulled in every direction and focusing on God becomes an uphill battle. But pray we must. Of all the disciplines of the faith, prayer and reading the Word must be diligently pursued.

A protracted fast and an honest emptying of yourself before God can have a very sobering effect on your healing process. Remember, we are the ones who moved, not God.

Restored to Spouse

If reconnecting with God seems like an uphill battle, restoration to our spouse presents itself as being an even more challenging pursuit. Restoration at this intimate level requires hard work. After all, many years of trust have been broken. The warning signs she might have pointed out to you that appeared along your reckless path were conveniently ignored. And now, as the innocent party, she is involuntarily removed from the church and society at large. This was my wife Dorselie's lot.

Dorselie is an excellent leader. Added to this quality/gift, she loves people. Making their day is a part of her DNA. But now, as a result of MY sin, she had to walk away from giving leadership to all the ministries in which she was involved. Having interacted with and given leadership to many women on a regular basis, she now felt a tremendous loss of ministry opportunities and experienced a greatly diminished circle of friends. If I had the power to do so, this would be one of the losses I would reverse.

It was very painful for me to see the remorse and sadness that engulfed her spirit as a result of my selfish behaviour. It devastated her. Her disruption from ministry and lack of interaction with her friends and community hurt me greatly. There were times when, against her will, she could not avoid meeting with members of our community. These moments caused embarrassment to resurface and stirred up her anger against me. These were stressful, emotional times. There is no way she could have prepared herself to cushion this blow she received.

Consequently, at the root of all this, her trust in me was badly shaken. It was sorely tried and tested. Whenever awkward meetings occurred, I bore the brunt of her humiliation. She would remind me of my selfish behaviour and my inability and/or short-sightedness to realize what this would do to her and our family. To say these were stressful and painful days would be an understatement. I have learnt afresh that forgiveness does not equal trust. Consequently, forgiveness came much easier than trusting again. Nonetheless, through my horrific behavior, Dorselie found it in her heart not just to forgive me, but also to restore her trust in me. In so doing, she was not just fulfilling an act, but rather demonstrating a permanent attitude. Her response to my sin was not just a testimony of grace, but also a statement that said she trusted God to be a better justice-maker than she was. By receiving me back into her confidence, she released her own right to get even and left all issues of fairness for God to work out. She is a remarkable woman of God!

I am thankful most of all for Dorselie's love for God and her Christian maturity, without which we probably would not have survived this ordeal. The way she battled this "storm" demonstrated to me the difference between theoretical and practical Christianity, and between maturity and immaturity. In time, I saw the love of Christ exude again from her. Consequently, my love, appreciation, and respect for her has grown exponentially. Her godly experience and Christ-like disposition afforded her the ability to see the big picture of marriage. She took seriously the "for better or for worse" part of her wedding vows, and remained faithful when the "for worse" seasons arrived. By truly forgiving me, she enhanced the quality of our lives and relationship. For all this and much more, I love her deeply.

Dorselie's personality and beautiful spirit have also been attested to outside of the home. She is, and always has been, a delightful person. This has been confirmed not just by her inner circle of friends and co-workers, but also by the hundreds of customers she has befriended over the years of her banking career—customers into whose lives she has had opportunities to make meaningful and lasting spiritual deposits.

A word of thanks is appropriate here to our many friends, far and near, who have prayed for us, counselled us, and stayed with us through this season of our lives. I specifically observed how supportive and protective Dorselie's friends have been. I am deeply indebted to these wonderful Christian women, who did not cease to love her through this season. You ladies have proved to be God's hands extended at a time when help was most needed. You are very special friends to us. God bless you!

Restored to My Children

As can be expected, my children were not prepared to receive this kind of news. Nonetheless, their response was very gracious and forgiving. As I sat with them individually, I sensed the type of love that could only have come from the solid friendships we have developed over the decades. I emphasize the word "friendship" over "parental relationship" because of an intentional transformation of our relationship that happened when they were in their late teens. Once they celebrated their eighteenth birthday, I let them know that we were transitioning to establishing a friendship as opposed to the default position we held as parents. They were given the privilege to call me by my first name and received the permission to interact, share, and converse with me as they would with their friends. This was a privilege granted to me by my father around the same period of my life. In return, I worked at passing on the same honour to my children, and it has never been abused or disrespected.

When our children were in their mid-teens, Dorselie and I made the "mistake" of asking them to honestly evaluate us as parents. Well, let's just say our grades were not the best. And in the "virtual comments" section of the report, it was clear that there was much need for improvement. However, we survived and were given the opportunity to correct our faults. Most important of all, they helped us to become better parents, and ultimately better friends.

Restored to Ministry—Is This Possible?

The question is frequently asked: Is it possible to restore a pastor who has sinned sexually? The answer probably depends on how we define restoration. Restoration can be seen as two

types: 1.) restoration to fellowship and community, and 2.),
restoration to pastoral ministry. When it comes to the first
instance, people are more ready to forgive and a lot more
willing to embrace and receive the pastor back to fellowship
and community. However, when it comes to restoration to
ministry, there seems to be a lot more hesitation and differing
views. There are at least three common schools of thought that
churches and leaders typically hold on to when it comes to
restoring a pastor back to the pulpit. Succinctly stated, they are
as follows:

1. **No restoration:** Some leaders believe that once a pastor
   has disqualified himself through sexual moral failure,
   he should be permanently removed from pastoring.
   The Scripture that is used to substantiate this standard
   is 1 Timothy 3. Here Paul sets out the requirements
   for leaders. In verse 2, he says, "Now the overseer (or
   pastor) must be above reproach, the husband of but one
   wife, temperate, (and) self-controlled…" In other words,
   his "proven observable conduct must be blameless in his
   marital life, family life, social life, and business life." The
   view advanced here is this: The pastor's sin will prevent
   him from ever being above reproach again. Therefore,
   his sin has ruined a blameless standing before the
   people to whom he will give pastoral leadership.[144]

2. **Immediate restoration:** The view purported here says
   that the pastor should be restored to ministry quickly.
   Once he has repented, he should be restored to fellowship with the church. To substantiate this view,
   they point to leaders in the Scripture who were used
   immensely by God after committing disqualifying
   sins. Biblical models cited to support this view include
   Moses, who murdered an Egyptian before leading

the Israelites to freedom, and David, who committed adultery and murder but was still mightily used by God to write many of the Psalms. Of course, the problem with this view of restoration is the fact that leaders are rushed back into leadership without time for new patterns of behaviour to be established.

3. **Deliberate restoration:** The argument advanced here is that restoration can and should occur: 1.) when the restoration is done deliberately, and when credibility can be restored through a season of learning and counselling; and 2.) when ample time is given to observe the fruit of repentance. Unlike the "no restoration" view, they believe that blamelessness can be restored. While all sins are a violation of the character of God, different levels of consequences need to be applied to each situation because each sin brings a different level of reproach upon Christ's church. It is therefore wise to acknowledge the fact that it takes years for a pastor to be trained for ministry, and in some cases, was indulging in sin for years. Consequently, it is not unreasonable to design a year or years of restoration, depending on the unique circumstances of each erring pastor.

The Reality of a Restoration Program

Restoration programs, I suspect, will vary in the way they are administered, depending on the denomination in question. The Pentecostal Assemblies of Canada (PAOC), of which I am a part, is a grace-based family. Over the decades of our existence, we have been very intentional in caring for and restoring fallen pastors. However, the nature of restorative ministry is private so for the sake of those involved, often the details and positive stories must remain unknown.

Restorative ministry is very commendable and is much appreciated by those recipients who have been restored as a result of this process. Coming alongside a fallen pastor is a practical way of saying we love you and want to see you reinstated first to God, next to your spouse and family, and then back to ministry. Of course, the purpose of walking a pastor through this rebuilding process is clearly intended to be restorative, even though at times it has not always felt this way.

Rev. Craig Burton is the Superintendent of the Eastern Ontario and Nunavut Districts in Canada. Speaking with him on this topic of restoration, he clearly articulated what the values of our fellowship are: "Candidates for restoration," he says, "must first be willing to acknowledge their violation of biblically based shared values, then a formal restoration program can be requested and granted. On occasion, a fallen credential holder will refuse to either acknowledge wrongdoing or fail to request formal restoration. In this event, a credential holder is restricted from continuing formal vocational ministry within our fellowship.

When a credential holder does however walk in repentance and good faith and requests formal restoration, the result is generally positive with the person completing their restorative journey and becoming available for future engagement in vocational ministry. This rarely involves their former employing church, however, there are many wonderful stories of ministry involvement for those who have completed a restoration program."

Practical Challenges of a Restoration Program

On occasion, restoration candidates may not complete their formal programs, and if this were to occur, they would not be accepted back into vocational ministry with the PAOC fellowship. As unfortunate as this may sound, there are a few reasons why this may occur.

First, the main challenge is simply that the period away from ministry and the deprivation of gainful employment is too long. In the minds of these pastors, what begins purposefully as a restorative goal, quickly degenerates into what seems to be a punitive "sentence".

Secondly, there is the reality of providing for the day-to-day needs of their families. When the decision to embark upon a restoration program has been made, pastors then have to look for a non-ministerial job. While this is obviously no fault of the Fellowship, if or when the shift to secular work is made, these pastors quickly become loyal to their new type of work. Consequently, by the time the restorative period is over, these pastors are then fairly established in their new form of employment and may be reluctant to make the transition back to ministry.

Thirdly, there is what I call the "blame and shame" issue that has the power to ostracize pastors from ministry and cause them to even question the "calling" that was placed on their lives.

Fourthly, pastors have expressed the feeling that the counselling received might not have been as helpful or as effective as they might have expected.

I am sure there are many more reasons why fallen pastors refuse to begin, or fail to complete, their restoration programs. But according to Romans 11:29 NIV, "...God's gifts and his call are irrevocable." As such, genuine care and compassion should be taken to ensure that none of these fallen pastors end up completely and permanently ostracized from ministry. A permanent departure from ministry would result in missed opportunities to share with colleagues what they would have learned during the time away from ministry. It would also be a missed opportunity to encourage and model for others what the grace of God can accomplish. This view is further expressed in a message in which the preacher shared these thoughts: 1.) Failure in the past does not nullify purpose in the future; and 2.) A broken heart is great preparation for healing broken lives.

Fallen pastors are still valuable workers in the Kingdom of God. And as such, I believe barriers to restoration need to be identified and steps to eradicate them need to be taken into serious consideration.

Restoration programs across the Pentecostal Assemblies of Canada are offered through our various districts, yet there is general alignment regarding the goals and purposes behind them. While we are not a perfect Fellowship, nor have we purported to be so, it is worthy of note, however, that we continue to revise and review our programs in order to better serve those who are walking through the hope-filled journey of restoration.

FOR REFLECTION AND INTROSPECTION

1. What regrets gnaw at your soul? Who in your life might be a safe person to talk to for reassurance of God's grace?

2. Are there signs in your life that restoration has occurred? Share what this looks like in reality with your friends.

3. Which of the gruelling questions listed in this chapter do you find very convicting and applicable to your present situation? What do you plan to do about this?

Chapter 10

DORSELIE'S STORY

"No test…that comes your way is beyond the course
of what others have had to face. All you need to
remember is that God will never let you down;
he'll never let you be pushed past your limit;
he'll always be there to help you come through it."

1 Corinthians 10:13 MSG

IT WAS ANOTHER week of church ministry with no unusual activities. The business of work at the office seemed normal with no pending signs of what would be revealed to me in the next few hours and days. Our Fall days of prayer, which fell between September 6–9, concluded that Friday evening. Colin was at the closing prayer meeting. As I reflected later, he did seem somewhat distracted and not his usual self. That being said, it was not unusual at times that after prayer meetings he would return to his office to tie up loose ends or care for unfinished business to end the work week. So I concluded that he was preoccupied with work-related assignments to which he needed to attend.

My friend and I were simply talking in the parking lot when Colin appeared and told me that he would be home late as he was heading off to a meeting. While this seemed a bit unusual for the time of night, I understood that this came with the Team Leader's territory and responsibilities, as there were times when meetings had to be scheduled according to the other party's availability. So I went home, prepared for bed, and promptly fell asleep before he returned home.

About 5:45 a.m. Saturday morning, he gently touched me and I awoke to hear him say, "Are you sleeping? The thing that I feared has come upon me." Immediately, I got a chilling sense in my stomach and soon my heart began to race and my body froze. In those brief moments, I instantly realized that what I was about to hear was not good news. So, I braced myself for the worst revelation. Over the next several minutes, he confessed that he had committed the sin of adultery, and it had come to light. This news left me numb and dumbfounded. Every emotion assailed me at once. I felt betrayed, enraged, angry, and disappointed. In asking for forgiveness, he also made it clear that he took full responsibility for his actions. He expressed remorse and regret for his deeds.

I could feel that my blood pressure had soared. I lost my speech for hours into days. I was broken-hearted and felt alone. It was so painful that I even found it difficult to pray.

Several emotions flooded my thoughts. Was I responsible for his actions? Should I have been more intimate? Should I have been more involved and cognizant of his daily activities? And on and on the questions arose and flooded my mind. Very few words were exchanged between us for several days following this revelation. I would look at him and feel the weight he was under for what he had done, and what making a public confession would do to him. He lost his appetite, and I could see the pounds falling from his body—not that he had any excess to shed.

I grieved for him. I ached for him. I cried for him. I prayed constantly that he would not crumble under such intense shame and embarrassment.

Next, I thought of our children, grandchildren, his siblings, his dad, the people at church, the hundreds of people that he had preached to, and the many he had counselled. The one thing I was very sure about was that he would have to be the one to share this news. I was too hurt and too ashamed to tell his story. I did call a dear friend of ours. We met at a plaza, and I shared with her what had happened. She was devastated and broke down in tears. She loves us both and felt the weight of what was still to come. She and her husband both prayed for us and stand with us to this very moment.

I felt certain that the entire world had heard the shameful and disappointing news. I thought about the hundreds of folks in our immediate community who were customers at the bank where I worked. I reflected on the many who I had shared my personal testimony with over the years, especially my three co-workers who had given their lives to Christ. I thought of the many people I had told about serving God and those I had invited to various special events at our church. I imagined that all my neighbours had heard the shocking news, so I only left our home if I had no other choice. On those rare occasions, I would open our front door and survey the neighbourhood. After looking east and west, if there was anyone in view, I quietly and quickly closed the door and tried again and again until there was no one in sight. If I was in a public place, I felt like everyone was looking at me and screaming "hypocrite!" I even imagined them mocking me behind my back.

I repeatedly asked God, "Why Omniscient? You knew that Colin would bring shame to You, the family, the church, our children, and to so many people. So why did You call him into ministry?" Even though in the past I never doubted God's call on Colin's life, now this revelation brought that into question. I recalled that several months prior to Colin being aware of God's call to full-time ministry, I felt a distinct consciousness of his calling from God. I did not share my impressions with him, but I kept wondering to myself if God was leading and calling him into full-time ministry, why had Colin not shared this with me? However, sometime later he shared and confirmed what I had been sensing from God.

The week leading up to the Sunday for the public confession, we agreed to share the news with some of the long-standing members of our congregation. Out of respect for them, we did not feel it would be right for them to hear it for the first time from the pulpit. We felt an obligation to share and ask for their forgiveness. This was a very difficult experience for both of us as Colin went to each family's home. My heart ached. Tears flowed. But at the end of those two days of going from house to house, I felt that he had made the right decision.

***

In early 1980, for several weeks during my lunch hour, I would drive to the church we attended, go up to the balcony, get down on my knees, and cry out to God concerning His plans for our lives. I felt quite strongly that Colin was being prepared for ministry. However, my false perception of the requirements of being a pastor's wife overwhelmed me. I felt unworthy. Sure, I loved God. I had been a Christian for decades. I was a Small Group Leader. I had led several people to a personal relationship with Christ; taught Sunday school; given leadership to Women's Ministry Groups; and was involved in other forms of ministry. I also love people; I always have. But despite all that, I still felt unworthy.

After several weeks of studying various biblical characters, which included Barnabas, I distinctly felt that God clearly impressed upon me that the role He had for me to fill would be that of an encourager. I was being called to love people genuinely and unconditionally. From that day on, I never questioned His purpose for my life. Instead I endeavoured to sincerely love and care for people as situations arose.

**

The Sunday of Colin's public confession, our three children, son-in-law, and a special friend from out of town attended both services to support us. I could feel the inevitable weight my husband was experiencing, having to stand before his congregation, confess his sin, and ask for their forgiveness in both services. As was expected, this came as a tremendous shock to the people. This was the very last thing they ever expected to hear from their pastor. Yet many appreciated his courage to stand before them. He openly shared in a lengthy letter his love for them, asking for their forgiveness and encouraging them to remain faithful to God who, unlike him, would never fail them. Together, in one accord, the congregation stood up and gave a rousing ovation for what was received as a genuine and sincere confession.

At the conclusion of both services, many parishioners lined up for hours afterwards to grieve with us and to assure us of their continued love, support, and prayers. It was a humbling experience and an outpouring of love and forgiveness. As to be expected, several left feeling disappointed, betrayed, and grieved, which was also an appropriate response. It was not surprising to learn that several negative statements were also made. In fact, a staff member saw me in a store a few months later and uttered some very unkind and hurtful words. I thanked her for her honesty and shared her disappointment. Another said he was not yet willing to forgive my husband, for he felt that "forgiveness is progressive". On a more positive note, for several weeks, many women visited with me, prepared meals, sent notes, and were very supportive. To all of you ladies, I am forever grateful for your outpouring of love, prayers, support, and kind deeds during that very difficult period.

A few weeks after his public confession, we attended one of the churches in Toronto. The title of the pastor's message that morning was, "Seasons Change". As I sat and listened, I knew that God had led us to that church, and consequently, the message was directed to me and to us as a couple. We drove home in silence, and for most of the forty-minute commute, we were both in silence as we each meditated on the message and knew in our own hearts that God had personally ministered to us that day. Now as I write, three years later, we still attend that church and have experienced much love and care from that body of believers.

I have tried to be open and honest when sharing with folks about my/our experience. In fact, I was asked to be a part of a panel of speakers at a Women's Meeting some time ago. I took the opportunity to share a portion of my journey up to that point. To my utter surprise, the response to my testimony made a few ladies feel safe to share their personal stories with me. This opened more doors to healing, as I was able to pray with, and for them, and to encourage them to continue on their spiritual journey with God. Several Scriptures have since been made clearer to me as I wrestled with it all. These have brought much healing and comfort to me during this season of my life. Romans 8:28 reminds me of this truth:

> "And we know that God causes everything to work together for the good of those who love God and are called according to his purpose for them." (NLT).

Another Scripture that has been especially helpful to me is 1 John 1:9:

> "…if we confess our sins to him, he is faithful and just to forgive us our sins and to cleanse us from all wickedness." (NLT).

These and many other Scriptures have encouraged and reassured me of God's mercy and His grace so richly bestowed upon us. Colin and I both believe that God's purpose for our ministerial lives is not yet over. Yes, we did give Satan the power to derail our relationship with God and get us off the track that was set before us. But as horrific as it has been, this much we are confident of: God's ultimate plan for our lives will prevail.

We have committed ourselves to the restoration process. We continue to love God, love each other, and redeem the time by preparing for the next chapter of our lives. At the centre of this journey, we have committed to spending more time in prayer and the Word and endeavouring to live out the truths therein.

Though long, our restoration journey has turned out to be of tremendous benefit to us. We received great counsel, support, and prayers from two qualified godly counsellors. Tough questions were posed, and we answered as honestly as we could.

Never once did they make us feel like we were being judged, or worse, condemned for our sin. At the same time, the reality of the consequences of our actions was made very clear. Of course, there were moments when pain and tears were inevitably experienced, but the times of refreshing that ensued more than compensated for those emotions as they edged us forward on our journey towards wholeness. I can now say from experience that I would strongly recommend this kind of open and honest godly counselling to anyone facing a similar situation.

Forgiveness, I have re-learnt is not an option. I must confess, however, that although I have fully forgiven my husband, at times the memory of what he did still raises its ugly head. It gets worse whenever I feel cut off from friendships and church activities that I once enjoyed and shared with so many women. This saddens me.

On one occasion, this was magnified when a pastor's wife said to me that if her husband were to be involved in a similar moral failure, she would not forgive him. I was quite surprised by her admission and felt sad about her understanding of God's grace and her inability to also forgive. Yes, I agree that this kind of behaviour is earth-wrenching for anyone. However, I am saddened that after all that God has done for us, we still have not learned to model genuine and unconditional forgiveness. I must say that I find such interactions and comments very grievous when expressed by "matured Christians".

Romans 3:23 NIV reminds me again of this truth:

"…all have sinned and fall short of the glory of God."

I married a godly man. He sinned and disappointed many. But he is still a man after God's own heart. He loves God and loves people. He always has. He looks out for the underdogs.

He is a good provider. He is my best friend. What he did does not define who he is. Not at all. We all are sinners in need of a loving and forgiving Saviour who is waiting for us to call on Him and ask Him to transform us into His image from the inside out.

Conversations with our adult children were, at first, quite painful, as well as surprisingly helpful. Each expressed their disappointment, and yet they were very supportive of us. As family members, we had many honest conversations with each other. And at the end of the day, they stood with us at every step of the way. They loved us because of their love for God and their understanding of who He is.

To our children, thank you for praying and loving us unconditionally. We are so very proud of each of you. We are blessed to be in your lives.

If, as you read these words, you realize that you have not been open and honest in your marriage or with someone, I appeal to you to deal with this situation while you have breath. I recommend you keep no secrets. Confess what you have done and ask God and those offended to forgive you. When this is done sincerely from your heart, healing virtue begins to flow. There is also no substitute for getting into the Word, meditating on it, and declaring God's promises over your life.

I have read several books that have been very helpful. I have listened to folks tell their personal stories. But most helpful of all has been God's Word and His promises for me, His child.

I do not know where you are in your personal journey: Maybe you have done wrong and you want to set it right; perhaps you yourself have been hurt deeply by someone. But no matter where you find yourself, there is always hope. All is not lost. *You will rise again.*

Through all I have experienced, the embarrassment and the pain, God has never let me down. He is faithful. He is true. He has been with me every step of the way. Loving me. Reminding me of His promises. Mending my heart in quiet moments. Turning my tears into joy. To Him be all glory and honour. AMEN!

Chapter 11
GRACE UNLIMITED

"For it is by grace you have been saved, through
faith—and this is not from yourselves, it is the gift of
God—not by works, so that no one can boast."

Ephesians 2:8-9 NIV

IF IT WEREN'T for grace, none of us would qualify for heaven. I have always been very cognizant of God's grace richly bestowed upon my life. But I must also confess that there were times when I was guilty of taking His grace for granted.

When I thought about an appropriate name to give to this book, the words of the great hymn "Grace Greater Than Our Sin", written by Julia H. Johnston (1849-1919), instantly came to mind. Johnston powerfully captured the concept of grace in the four stanzas of her hymn. "She spoke of sin and despair that threatens the soul. She spoke of a dark stain that we cannot hide. But she also lifted up the cross of Christ as the remedy for our sin—as the prescription to relieve us of our guilt."[145] It is the type of grace that not only pardons guilty sinners, but also cleanses us within. What an awesome attribute of God she tapped into!

While reflecting on the words of this hymn, I realized once again that this kind of selfless love can only come from Almighty God. Therefore I invite you to meditate with me on the words of this hymn.

> Marvellous grace of our loving Lord,
> grace that exceeds our sin and our guilt!
> Yonder on Calvary's mount outpoured,
> there where the blood of the Lamb was spilt.

> *Chorus*
> Grace, grace, God's grace,
> grace that will pardon and cleanse within;
> grace, grace, God's grace,
> grace that is greater than all our sin!

> Sin and despair, like the sea waves cold,
> threaten the soul with infinite loss;
> grace that is greater, yes, grace untold,
> points to the refuge, the mighty cross.

> Dark is the stain that we cannot hide.
> What can avail to wash it away?
> Look! There is flowing a crimson tide,
> brighter than snow you may be today.

> Marvellous, infinite, matchless grace,
> freely bestowed on all who believe!
> You that are longing to see His face,
> will you this moment His grace receive?

Throughout the Word of God, we see numerous recipients of God's grace. Among Christians, it is our belief that grace is the free and unmerited favour of God as manifested in the salvation of sinners and the bestowal of blessings. Whole books have been written endeavouring to explain this awesome attribute of God, and yet we find ourselves humbled whenever we experience His Grace pursuing us.

But grace, I have found, is an attribute of God that can be abused, and consequently, we run the risk of possibly receiving it in vain. The word vain means useless, ineffective, unproductive or of no value. When the Apostle Paul graciously appealed to the Corinthians, in 2 Corinthians 6:1, not to receive the gift of God's grace in vain, this obvious question surfaced in my mind. How can we receive God's grace in vain, especially when He is giving it? And once acknowledged, is it really possible for the grace of God to be proved ineffective or fruitless?

I believe, like the Corinthians, we can receive the grace of God in vain when our sinful practice does not measure up to the profession of our faith. We find ourselves acting like immature Christians who ask the question: "Why be good when you know in advance you will be forgiven?" That's a dangerous way to live!

Therefore, we need to be reminded that while God's grace is so unlimited that it can cover any sin, it must be received sincerely and with a feeling of remorse for the wrongdoing. The opposite of this response is to see grace as a way of glossing over our sins or excusing them away on the basis of God's promise of forgiveness. Understand that when we truly comprehend what God has done for us, then out of sincere gratitude, we strive to live lives that are worthy of His grace and love. This is when we wholeheartedly agree with Paul when he says it is the grace of God that "...teaches us to say "No" to ungodliness and worldly passions, and to live self-controlled, upright, and godly lives in this present age..." (Titus 2:12 NIV). A realization of this truth causes us to spend our days trying to fathom, not exploit, God's grace.

Among some of my favourite examples of grace richly bestowed upon biblical characters, the following stand out in my mind.

Ruth the Moabite

By far, this is one of my favourite biblical characters. I find her story quite intriguing. I love this book for many reasons, but mainly because I see God's amazing grace displayed in each chapter. The book of Ruth is brilliantly written, highlighting some powerful themes: faithfulness, kindness, integrity, protection, prosperity, and blessing. In essence, this is a story of God's grace in the midst of difficult circumstances that occurred at a time in history when people lived to please themselves, not God. (Judges 17:6). God graciously permitted a broken Moabite widow to find refuge, hope, and fulfillment through the love, compassion, and grace of a wealthy and influential farmer from Bethlehem. I recall preaching a four-part series on the Book of Ruth that dealt with four themes, each representing what transpired chronologically in its four chapters: Weeping, Working, Waiting, Wedding.

The Apostle Paul

His conversion and subsequent call to ministry have no biblical parallel. Paul led a tumultuous life full of high highs and low lows. But in the midst of all this, the grace of God was evidently present throughout every season of his life. In 2 Corinthians 12, for example, we see Paul pleading with God to take away a thorn in his flesh. God's response to him was simply this: "My grace is sufficient for you, for my power is made perfect in weakness." (2 Corinthians 12:9 NIV).

Although God did not remove Paul's affliction, He demonstrated His power and grace through Paul's weaknesses and limitations. This grace prevailed through the many trials Paul endured. Like Paul, when we go through the storms of life, we too can look back and testify to this truth: God's grace truly is sufficient to meet all our needs; His unmerited favour always comes to our rescue.

The Apostle Peter

Probably one of Peter's biggest regrets in life, no doubt, was denying Jesus three times on the night before He was crucified. But even in Peter's season of regret and remorse, God richly lavished His grace upon him. How? In Mark 16, we are told the story of the three women who went to anoint Jesus' body after it was placed in a tomb. A young man dressed in a white robe informed the women that Jesus was no longer in the tomb. He had risen! He went on to instruct them as follows: "...go, tell his disciples **and Peter**, 'He is going ahead of you into Galilee.'" (Mark 16:6-7, emphasis mine). Isn't it so gracious of Jesus to specifically request that Peter be notified of His resurrection? Jesus knew that Peter was tormented by the fact that he had failed Him in His most crucial hour of need. As such, by singling out Peter, Jesus wanted him to know that despite his actions, He was going to graciously heal and restore their relationship.

Post-resurrection, as recorded in John 21:15-18, Jesus had a conversation with Peter on the beach—a conversation that exhibited a lot of love and grace. Here, we see Jesus reinstating Peter and entrusting him with the all-important task of feeding His lambs, taking care of His sheep, and feeding His sheep. Recall with me that this was the same disciple to whom

Jesus had said: "Simon, Simon, Satan has asked to sift all of you as wheat. But I have prayed for you, Simon, that your faith may not fail. And when you have turned back, strengthen your brothers." (Luke 22:31-32 NIV). This is the same disciple who had vowed he would never betray Jesus, even though Jesus had clearly predicted his denial. "I tell you the truth...before the rooster crows twice you yourself will disown me three times." (Mark 14:30 NIV). And of course, Peter did. But it was not the end of Peter's story; Jesus graciously restored him. He went on to be mightily used by God on the Day of Pentecost and beyond.

Looking back on my life, I too can truly testify that the love and grace of God have always pursued me. Shortly after my moral failure was revealed, I felt strangely comforted by two thoughts: 1.) Even though many were disappointed in me (and rightly so), and even though many others wanted to put some distance between us, like Peter, I knew and felt that Jesus still loved me; and 2.) I also knew that God would deal with me graciously.

What follows are three life-changing experiences in which God's grace, mercy, and loving kindness were obviously displayed. My purpose for sharing these stories is to reinforce the fact that God's grace is not only unlimited in its scope, but it invariably shows up in many aspects of life and ministry.

Let me begin with a test of my faith that God permitted me to have shortly after He called me to prepare for ministry.

First Year Training—"Off Campus"

Less than four weeks into my first year of Bible College training, it was discovered that my retina was partially detached—not just in one eye, but in both. My failing vision was beginning to impede my driving. I can recall a situation in which my distorted vision caused me to make a defensive response to what seemingly was shaping up to be a head-on collision. This scare prompted me to have my eyes checked. I was expecting the visit to be a quick and easy fix, but what lay ahead of me was anything but quick and easy. What I thought was going to be a routine check-up, turned out to be an eight-month-long ordeal.

After being checked by several physicians and medical students, I was told that 95% of the retina in my left eye was detached. And, if that revelation wasn't alarming and scary enough, I also learned that approximately 60% of the retina in the right eye was also detached. This serious diagnosis meant that they needed to operate immediately in order to avoid blindness in the left eye.

The first four-and-a-half-hour operation was not a 100% successful. Consequently, I was informed that they needed to operate on the right eye sooner than was previously expected in case it got worse and/or the vision did not return in my left eye.

Once the reality of what was happening dawned upon me, a number of thoughts and questions instantly flooded my mind: What if I never see again? Why this timing? Could the doctors do a temporary fix until spring so that I could finish out my first year of Bible College? What would others think about me and the claim I had made about the call of God on my life to prepare for ministry? (Indeed a few of my friends back home in Windsor, Ontario did question my calling due to this serious disruption in my health.) By God's grace, however, these thoughts and questions didn't destroy my faith;

conversely, they helped me to firmly establish in my mind that while this was obviously not God's doing, He certainly permitted it in order to accomplish what only He could in my life. Today I refer to this experience as First Year Bible College, off campus.

A few weeks after my first surgery, I underwent a second on my right eye. But as fate would have it, I was at that point deprived of total vision for a number of weeks. My head had to remain bandaged mainly to avoid any temptation to scratch my eyes, which would run the risk of infection. So night was dark and day was also like night. However, not being able to see made my other senses much keener. I learned to quickly detect the voices of my visitors and settled in to telling my story over and over again. On the positive side, on the seventeenth day of hospitalization, the Holy Spirit clearly impressed upon me that I would be out of college for the year, but I should not worry as He was in full control of this situation. The reassurance that God had orchestrated this helped me to adopt a more positive attitude towards my illness and gave me a boldness to share my faith with all who came to sympathize with me. So while my visitors felt the need to comfort me, I felt very empowered to minister to them in return.

Anxious Moments in the Camp

After the third hospitalization and very little hope of my sight returning, my faith was put to the test. The recovery of my sight was proving to be a much longer exercise than I had envisioned. I ended up undergoing five operations over a period of two months. By this point, I was understandably quite concerned about what was happening and seriously speculating about what this all meant for my vision going forward. Especially unsettling was the fact that a few bubbles of fluid had formed between the retina and my left eye. This posed the danger of the retina being pushed off at anytime—a situation that kept the medical team quite alert. I was under the care of a highly skilled physician, Dr. Moffatt. He had an impressive track record of performing more than 200 surgeries annually to reattach detached retinas. But my case was causing him some concern. I recall him coming to my room very early each morning and anxiously checking to see whether the fluid on the left eye had disappeared or at least was decreasing.

After a lengthy discussion, a decision was made to perform laser surgery in a bid to correct this issue; this would be my fifth surgery. Just prior to the operation, I mustered up the courage to ask Dr. Moffatt what would happen to my vision if this surgery was unsuccessful.

I will never forget his response to me. He said: "You are the Bible College student, old boy, you tell me!" Needless to say that was not the response I was expecting—and truth be told, it was not helpful in stilling my frayed nerves. Yes, I was a Bible College student. Yes, my faith was supposed to be strong. Yes, I probably should have committed this response to prayer at that very moment and represented Christ better before the doctor. But as I stood there contemplating the reality of not being able to see again, the primary thought and emotion I experienced was fear. A deep horror engulfed my heart in that moment.

My hope for a successful recovery was challenged by the unknown future. I encouraged myself with the thought that even if I were never to see again, I would not let that deter me from becoming a pastor. I also consoled myself with the fact that at the age of 33, I had memorized so much Scripture that if the worst were to happen, I would be able to preach without notes. While this sounded good in theory, my mind was bombarded with the thoughts of all the loved ones I would never see again, all the beautiful sights I would only be able to imagine, and the inconvenience I would cause my wife and close relatives in having to care for me and aid in my mobility.

For what seemed like a very long period of time, these thoughts triumphed over faith. Nonetheless, in time, I felt that God's grace was going to be more than sufficient to ultimately alleviate my fears.

By God's grace, my faith received a major boost one morning. While I was praying and asking God to heal me and send me home, I sensed the Holy Spirit impress this on my heart: "Colin, the doctors will do their best to fix your eyes, but your vision will not return. But after they are finished, I will touch your eyes and restore your sight." What a solid word this was! I received it as one would relish good news from a far land. I grabbed hold of it as one holding on for dear life. It was an awesome God moment for me.

While there would be yet an additional four to six months of hospitalization and home care ahead of me, I never lost sight of that "I and Thou" moment with God. After Dr. Moffatt did the fifth operation on my eyes, I boldly told him that he would never operate on my eyes again. I thanked him for all that he had done and by faith added that the Great Physician would complete the work He began in me. A smile crept across his face; one I interpreted as saying to me: "Well, old boy, I wish I could believe the truth of your statement of faith, but my vast medical experience in this specialized field has taught me differently. Good luck to you."

The Miracle

Weeks later, I was finally sent home to Peterborough and placed under the care of another physician. The fluid on the retina was still a grave concern, even though it had neither increased nor decreased in weeks. After about five or six months of home care, I was able to see objects in a blurred manner. This was wonderful progress to me. I had gone from the possibility of not seeing again to now being able to detect objects and people. Glory to God! As the months went on, I was able to decipher words on a page, but they all appeared in a Z-like manner. But again, this gave me tremendous hope that I might regain at least some vision in the future. And then it happened!

One morning while I was home alone and trying to read my Bible, I tilted it in the normal fashion that afforded me the best position from which to read. All of a sudden, the words on the page were transformed from a Z-like shape into perfectly normal printed words! I no longer had to tilt the page to compensate for the twist each word had. In that state of awe, I quickly put down the Bible and picked up a book with a finer print. To my delight, the words were also straight and easy to recognize. Still not totally convinced of what was happening to me, I pulled out a concordance with about an 8-point font size. As I attempted to read, I sensed this rebuke from the Holy Spirit: "What are you doing, Colin? Did I not tell you how your sight was going to be restored?" It was that reprimand that made me realize I was experiencing a miraculous touch from God!

I leapt out of my chair and began dancing around the house, praising God and thanking Him for His miraculous healing power. Next, I called my wife, Dorselie, who was at work and told her what had happened. She could not wait to get home to witness for herself the truth of this phenomenon. As soon as she got home, we took the opportunity to give God thanks for what He had done!

A little while after my miraculous healing, I was sent back to Dr. Moffatt for my regular check-up. I will never forget how puzzled he was that day when he checked my eyes. Because he had checked my eyes dozens of times before, I knew the exact routine he followed during his examination. His first order of business was to check the problematic areas of my eyes. As such, he would skip over examining the areas where the retina sat well and give priority to checking the problem area where the fluid had settled. But on that notable day, he frantically checked every part of my eye, and then repeatedly checked and rechecked the problematic spot until he couldn't remain silent any more.

"Hmm, there is no more fluid on the retina, and it is sitting nicely on the back of the eye!" I don't remember what else he said, for he was a man of few words. But I do recall him saying that he would tell my optometrist to write a prescription for my new glasses, followed by the best news of all: "Old boy, you can return to doing whatever activities you did before your operations." My response? Glory to God!

While this was awesome news for me, I can still see in my mind's eye (no pun intended) the fate of at least two friends that I made during my long stay on the fifth floor of Toronto General Hospital. We were all hospitalized for the same problem, and we all hoped and believed that our vision would return. But one woman did not have as positive an experience as mine. After approximately ten months of hospitalization, she was still wearing dark glasses because of how sensitive her eyes were to light. As I watched her in the waiting room, I felt sad but also humbled by the grace and favour I had received from the hand of God. My only response in that moment was to give thanks to God.

Prison Ministry

In the early 1990s, I was involved in doing prison ministry at two penitentiaries in Kingston, Ontario. Over my years of pastoring, I have had the privilege of seeing several dangerous incarcerated men come to know God as Saviour in at least six prisons in two different countries. Consequently, as you can imagine, many stories of God's saving grace abound. I have always been amazed at how imprisoned men and women come to experience freedom in Christ, while "free citizens" continue to live imprisoned lives. It all comes down to each person's decision as to whether or not they would acknowledge and accept Jesus Christ as their Lord and Saviour. Even now as I type this, I am wrestling with whether I should share another glorious experience I had while speaking at a prison in another county. But for now that will have to take second place to the story I will share about an inmate I ministered to in Collins Bay Penitentiary. In order to protect his privacy I will refer to him by the fictitious name of Jimmy Wilson.

Jimmy was among approximately 30 inmates who attended one of the services held in Collins Bay Penitentiary back in the fall of 1992. As usual, after my salvation message that day, I gave the opportunity for the men to accept Christ into their hearts. A few of them responded affirmatively, and our ministry team proceeded to pray with them individually. When I got to Jimmy, who did not respond to the salvation call, I asked him what would hinder him from accepting Christ into his heart. This was his response: "I have spent so much time in prison that I don't know how to live outside of this institution. So when I have completed serving my time, I plan to go across the street and commit a crime that would bring me back into this prison." Needless to say, in my time of doing prison ministry, I had heard just about every reason why inmates were not prepared to give their lives to God, but this one was different. I felt Jimmy's disillusionment with life, and his struggle to surrender to imprisonment for the rest of his life.

A boldness overtook me as I became angry at Satan for keeping this man in his mid-forties in bondage over these many years.

I challenged Jimmy to believe that whatever his crime was, God's grace and forgiveness were more than sufficient to help change the trajectory of his life. And so I presented Jimmy with an unusual challenge; one I was willing and prepared to follow through with. I told him that if he would sincerely give his heart to the Lord, I would commit to follow up and work with him to see him reintegrated into society, which included finding him accommodation and a job.

Jimmy accepted my offer and prayed a prayer for salvation that moved him from fear to faith in God. The instant change of his countenance revealed he had experienced the saving grace of God! I took out one of my ministry cards, handed it to him, and gave him some specific instructions: "Call me when you get out of here, and I will meet with you to begin the reorientation process back to society." I left the penitentiary that day marvelling at how the grace of God works and continued with my ministry as usual.

Three months later, when I had just about forgotten the promise I had made to Jimmy, I received a phone call late one night. The person on the other end of the phone said: "Hello Pastor, this is Jimmy. I can see you from where I am, but I just wanted you to know that I am out of prison." What might have been good news for Jimmy suddenly became quite a concern for me. An ex-convict was calling me from someone's home, late at night, and was in such close proximity to the church's parsonage that he could actually see that I was in the kitchen. However I was going to deal with this situation, one thing was abundantly clear; I would not be in a hurry to share this conversation with my wife—at least not at that hour of the night.

We got through the night uneventfully. The following day I met with Jimmy, and he filled me in on all that he had accomplished since being out of prison for a few days. He was able to secure some temporary housing with some old friends and had some pocket money he had earned from doing small jobs while in prison. As a culmination of the things we talked about, I invited Jimmy to attend church and promised him I would not be sharing his story with anyone. Even now as I type, I remember watching Jimmy attend church Sunday after Sunday. He was always dressed in his black t-shirt and black pants. He would sit in the same pew, and he appeared to always enjoy the service. Unfortunately, I don't think anyone ever befriended Jimmy, but he would smile whenever I would make mention of inmates I had the privilege of leading to the Lord.

My friendship with Jimmy grew to the point where he felt he could share his total life story with me. One day he said to me, "Pastor, I want to meet with you to share my story, but we will need a lot of time." I decided to set apart two hours one Saturday afternoon to meet with him at my office. Except for a function the women were attending in the basement of the church, there were no other activities happening in the building that day. Jimmy arrived as scheduled and began to share with me what his life had been like from childhood right up to adulthood.

Jimmy's Life's Story

After two hours of sharing some horrific things he had experienced in life, Jimmy paused only to shed some tears, and to convince himself that I was indeed willing to continue listening to him without being so scared that I would cut the meeting short. Around the mid-point of our visit, one of the ladies came up to my office with two plates of food. This caring gesture was truly God-sent because our meeting ended up lasting for over five hours! At the end of our meeting, Jimmy wiped his brow, let out a sigh, and said, "There! Finally, somebody had the courage to listen to my life's story in its entirety! Pastor I have tried over the years to share my story with others, but every time I got to the scary parts, they would stop me and promise to continue the meeting at a later date. But they never did!"

If you can imagine what might possibly take over five hours to share, you would know that his life's journey was a very sad and painful one. His experiences consisted of many abuses, abandonments, fights, broken relationships, excessive alcohol and drug usage, and everything else that would send a clear message to a young man that he was not wanted, loved, or valued! As Jimmy shared his story, I clearly understood why others who tried to help him in the past became fearful and asked him to stop. I found out that Jimmy had a temper, which when triggered by his short fuse, literally led to murder.

He was highly intolerant of people who bullied others. He disdained men who took advantage of women. And yet despite this "fight for the underdog" attitude, Jimmy had ironically committed two separate murders that procured him over 30 years of imprisonment. This irony was most evident when he shared with me how and why these murders occurred. But I will spare you the horrific details of this part of his story. Suffice to say, however, God graciously rescued Jimmy from totally shipwrecking his life.

Fast Forward

The grace of God is life changing. It overlooks all our filth and unworthiness and pursues us wholeheartedly and unapologetically. The grace, love, and salvation of God give us all a clean slate no matter how dark a history we may have had. Jimmy went from being a hardened criminal to believing that God could use him to lead others to Christ. His newfound relationship with God ultimately gave him the desire to go to Bible College to train to become a pastor. Upon completion of his studies, his plan was to go back to his community to share the good news of salvation with his people.

That was Jimmy's plan when he left the church. I don't know where he is today, and I don't know if he was able to fulfill his life's quest; but I do believe that Jimmy was a recipient of God's saving grace and protective power. His invitation to allow Jesus to be Lord of his life made a qualitative difference in his new way of living. He could honestly testify that "… anyone who belongs to Christ has become a new person. The old life is gone; a new life has begun!" (2 Corinthians 5:17 NLT). Glory to God!

We Will All Live Forever

One of the things that has occupied my thoughts over the last little while is how fleeting life is and how unpredictable our future is. No one has the luxury of determining how long they will live *on planet earth*. Recently, while speaking to a group of male teenagers, I made this radical statement: You will all live forever! The shocked look that occupied their faces clearly conveyed to me that they had never heard nor thought about this before. After explaining my reason for this revelation, I encouraged them to make wise and good decisions (including giving their lives to Jesus) with every new day that is given to them.

We are eternal beings. Phase one of life is lived within human bodies; phase two begins when our spirits depart from our clay jars. No one knows how many days God has given us for phase one. As such, it behoves us to wisely prepare for phase two of our eternity. One of the reasons why we are given today as a gift is to ensure that we do not take the present grace of God for granted. Proverbs 19:21 (NLT) reminds us of this sobering truth: "You can make many plans, but the Lord's purpose will prevail." So true!

Our Unique Journeys

Life is a journey. And the unique situations that each of us will experience are designed to prepare us to meet our Lord upon the conclusion of our earthly lives. Life happens. Our best plans fail. Many of our hopes and aspirations never come to fruition. The impact that we had hoped to make upon our family, our community, and our world may turn out to be less impressive than we had anticipated. But through all the ups and downs of life, the predictable and the unpredictable, the accomplishments and impacts we have made or failed to make, God's grace has always been present. God's grace has always pursued us. And, hopefully, God's ultimate plan for our lives will be actualized.

We all strive to live out and live up to many biblical themes, the first of which is salvation—the surrendering of our lives to God and pledging that we will be faithful and love Him with our whole hearts, minds, and strength. After we are born again, we endeavour to live lives that are worthy of the calling that has been placed upon us as Children of the Most High God. To this end, we strive to fulfill the Great Commission, to be obedient, to forgive, to be gracious and loving, to be Christlike in all our ways, to be good Christian models, to care for the poor, to pass on a godly heritage to our children, etc. Yes, there are indeed many themes in the Bible, and these themes form the fabric of what Christian living is all about. But when I stop to reflect on life on planet earth and the brevity of our years, I realize that there is a need to keep the main thing in life as the main thing—and that for me can be summed up this way: **Love God and love people**. In so doing, we glorify and enjoy Him as we worship Him and serve the people He has placed in our community.

Conversely, the way my life has unfolded, specifically over the last few years, can be seen as a bit of a deviation from fulfilling my God-ordained purpose for living. This is precisely one of the reasons for writing this book. It is my hope that my experiences will be seen as a stark reminder to all of us not to receive the grace of God in vain. For unless God's love and grace continue to pursue us in this life, we are running a losing race. After all, it is God who created us, saved us, loves us, and continues to prepare us to spend the rest of eternity with Him. It therefore behoves us to reciprocate His love and receive His grace with thanksgiving.

In Ephesians Chapters 2 and 3, we are reminded of the fact that we can brag about nothing—not status, accomplishments, wealth, power, or influence. In short, we can brag about nothing this world counts as attributes of success. Our default system led us to major in disobedience and sin, and steered us in the ways of the devil. But our God, who is rich in mercy, loves us so much that He devised a plan to save us. This salvation is not a reward for anything good we have done, but rather, it is all about His grace; the unmerited favour of God.

This is why we can't take credit for our salvation, let alone boast about anything we have done. For it is God who first took the initiative and gave us this wonderful gift! He "raised us up with Christ and seated us with him in the heavenly realms…in order that in the coming ages he might show the incomparable riches of his grace expressed in his kindness to us in Christ Jesus." (Ephesians 2:6-7, NIV). The Apostle Paul calls this a mysterious plan of God that was kept secret from the beginning but now has become known to everyone who chooses to believe in him. (Ephesians 3:9, NIV). Consequently, because of how rich He was in mercy, God loved us even though we were dead because of our sins, and gave us life when He raised Christ from the dead.

In Conclusion

Permit me to reiterate the main purpose for sharing my journey.

During this unplanned "time out" from ministry, work, leadership, and responsibilities, I was afforded the time to take a fresh look at how my life has unfolded. You may recall I began by identifying a traumatic classroom experience that laid a shaky foundation upon which I built my adult life. From there, I talked about the fall-out of what happened when sinful secrets were revealed. This led to a public confession to hundreds of people who I loved and had the privilege of caring for their spiritual lives.

Next I did a detailed look at Psalm 51. Learning from David's sin helped me to deal with mine. What a wonderful healing experience that was. I personally felt renewed by God's love, mercy, and grace. It aided me to take the next necessary steps to re-discover who I am and what I have become.

To accomplish this feat, I relied on the Holy Spirit to restore and renovate my heart back to the place where I once enjoyed intimacy with God. During this process, I read many books, received a lot of godly counsel, and spent time in fasting, prayer, and asking many friends and colleagues to forgive me. I also learned to forgive myself and accept God's forgiveness of my sins. Armed with the memories of my eye health challenge, and with the testimony of Jimmy's salvation and transformation, I was convinced afresh that God's mercies and grace are truly new every morning. This in turn propelled me to keep my head up, forge forward, and press on toward the mark for the prize of the high calling of God in Christ Jesus.

No one emerges from this type of humiliating experience the same. Impossible! The whole point of submitting to a restoration program is, in itself, a stark reminder of at least two things: 1.) I was broken and needed God's grace to make me whole again; and 2.) I will never again take for granted the privilege God gave to me to be His voice to the lost. Today I can testify to the fact that time has healed many wounds and has given me the opportunity to rise again.

For me, to be pursued by grace is to be followed, persistently sought out, protected, and continually loved and cherished by my Heavenly Father. It is to experience forgiveness, kindness, mercy, and encouragement as someone who is undeserving of God's favour and goodness. It is to be ever cognizant of the fact that the God who loves me unconditionally has given me yet another chance to reciprocate His love for me. In short, to be pursued by grace is to be constantly reminded that God created me to have fellowship with Him for all eternity.

So, to my many friends and all who read this testimony, my prayer for you is that you will learn from my sin and degradation about what God truly requires of you, and so avoid the schemes and devices of the evil one. Love God wholeheartedly. Worship Him passionately. Serve Him unswervingly. Represent Him faithfully. Proclaim Him unapologetically.

Remember and reflect on this word: "God saved you by his grace when you believed. And you can't take credit for this; it is a gift from God. Salvation is not a reward for the good things we have done, so none of us can boast about it. For we are God's masterpiece. He has created us anew in Christ Jesus, so we can do the good things he planned for us long ago." (Ephesians 2:8-10 NLT).

Titus also reminds us of this truth: "...the grace of God has appeared that offers salvation.... It teaches us to say 'No' to ungodliness and worldly passions, and to live self-controlled, upright, and godly lives in this present age." (Titus 2:11-12 NIV).

With these scriptural truths in mind, let us be intentional in clothing ourselves with humility and be grateful to God for His love. Through His relentless pursuit of grace, we have become recipients of this marvellous gift of salvation; a plan that could only have been devised by our Heavenly Father, who loves us unconditionally.

Jude, Jesus' half brother, gives us what I call a fitting closing thought of what I believe it means to be ultimately pursued by grace. He writes, "To him who is able **to keep you from falling** and to present you before his glorious presence **without fault** and with great joy—to the only wise God our Saviour be glory, majesty, power, and authority through Jesus Christ our Lord, before all ages, now and forevermore! Amen." (Jude 24-25, NIV, emphasis mine).

Let me share one last scripture that accurately captures the reason for my journey being so restorative. I am a recipient of God's mercy and grace.

The Apostle Paul has always been a favourite biblical character of mine, probably because I can see similarities in some aspects of his ministry and life's journey. In mentoring the young pastor Timothy, Paul reveals a truth to him that I too can identify with. He begins by saying this: "Here is a trustworthy saying that deserves full acceptance: Christ Jesus came into this world to save sinners—**of whom I am the worst.**" (emphasis mine). Obviously, while this is not something I am proud of, it perfectly describes me.

I am, nonetheless, also grateful that I can concur with what he goes on to say. "But for that very reason **I was shown mercy** so that in me, the worst of sinners, Christ Jesus might display his unlimited patience as an example for those who would believe in him and receive eternal life." (1 Timothy 1:15-16 NIV, emphasis mine).

On all the winding roads of life I have travelled, His grace, love and forgiveness have always pursued me. May this unfailing love always lead us to surrender to His gracious pursuit. And yes, while His grace is indeed unlimited, may we never be found guilty of taking this unmerited favour for granted. Glory to God!

FOR REFLECTION AND INTROSPECTION

1. In which area(s) of your life have you experienced God's grace lavished upon you? If you are comfortable in doing so, tell your life story.

2. What does it mean to receive the grace of God in vain? Are you guilty of this practice? If so, stop and ask God to forgive you.

3. Having read my story, what steps have you taken in order to avoid experiencing a moral failure? Do you have a better understanding of who you are? Have you sought out an accountability partner?

REFERENCES

Introduction
1   Dallas Willard, *Renovation of the Heart: Putting on the Character of Christ* (Colorado Springs, CO: NavPress, 2012), 222.

Chapter 1: My Foundational Years
2   Funk and Wagnalls, *Canadian College Dictionary* (Markham, ON: Harper and Row Publishers, Inc., 1986), Definition of the word "rod", 1164.
3   These were some of my primary school teachers who taught at St. Stephen's Scots School in Guyana back in the early 60s. Names have been changed to protect their identities.
4   Gary L. McIntosh and Samuel D. Rima, *Overcoming the Dark Side of Leadership* (Michigan: Baker Books, 2007), 174.
5   Ibid, 28.
6   Ibid, 70.
7   Ibid, 91.
8   Ibid, 153, 168.
9   Ibid, 217.
10   Milan and Kay Yerkovich, *How We Love* (New York: Water Brook Press, 2016), 50.

Chapter 2: When Secrets Are Revealed
11   Arnold R. Fleagle and Donald A. Lichi, *Broken Windows of the Soul* (Chicago, Illinois: Wing Spread Publishers, 2011), 68, 69.
12   NIV Life Application Study Bible, Notes, 478.
13   Andy Stanley, *Enemies of the Heart* (New York: Multnomah Books, 2011), 102-103.

14   Rosaria Champagne Butterfield, *Openness Unhindered* (Pittsburgh, PA: Crown and Covenant Publications, 2016), 75.

15   Ibid, 201.

16   Jordan B. Peterson, *12 Rules for Life: An Antidote to Chaos* (Toronto, ON: Penguin Random House Canada, 2018), 211.

17   Ibid, 215.

18   Ibid, 212.

19   Ibid, 228.

20   Willard, *Renovation of the Heart*, 35-36.

21   Ray Carroll, *Fallen Pastor: Finding Restoration in a Broken World* (Folsom, CA: Civitas Press, 2011), 110.

22   Ibid, 175.

Chapter 3: Public Confession

23   Pickering Pentecostal Church, also known as *The Gathering Place*, is located at 1920 Bayly Street, Pickering, ON, Canada. www.ppclife.ca.

24   Ray Pritchard, "How Much Sin Will God Forgive," last modified January 30, 2011, https://www.keepbelieving.com/sermon/how-much-sin-will-god-forgive/.

25   Earl and Sandy Wilson, et al., *Restoring the Fallen: A Team Approach to Caring, Confronting and Reconciling* (Downer's Grove, IL: InterVarsityPress, 1997), 81.

Chapter 4: #MeToo and the Church

26   *NLT Study Bible, 1 Chronicles 12:32a.*

27   *NIV Life in the Spirit Study Bible,* (Grand Rapids, Michigan: Life Zondervan Publishing Company, 2003), Commentary on 1 Chronicles 12: 32a, 587.

28   Alyssa Milano, "Twitter", last modified October 15, 2017, https://twitter.com/alyssa_milano/status/919659438700670976?lang=en.

29   Jodi Kantor and Megan Twohey, "Harvey Weinstein Paid Off Sexual Harassment Accusers for Decades," *The New York Times,* last modified October 5, 2017, https://www.nytimes.com/2017/10/05/us/harvey-weinstein-harassment-allegations.html.

30   Riley Griffin, Hannah Recht, and Jeff Green, "#MeToo: One Year Later," *Bloomberg*, last modified October 5, 2018, https://www.bloomberg.com/graphics/2018-me-too-anniversary/.

31   "History and Vision," *me too*, accessed January 18, 2019, https://metoomvmt.org/about/#history.

32   Griffin, Recht, and Green, "#MeToo: One Year Later".

33   Ibid.

34   Joshua Pease, "The sin of silence: The epidemic of denial about sexual abuse in the evangelical church," *The Washington Post*, last modified May 31, 2018, https://www.washingtonpost.com/news/posteverything/wp/2018/05/31/feature/the-epidemic-of-denial-about-sexual-abuse-in-the-evangelical-church/?utm_term=.c476c508d2e4.

35   Associated Press, "Tallying Sexual Abuse by Protestant Clergy," *The New York Times*, last modified June 15, 2007, https://www.nytimes.com/2007/06/15/us/15protestant.html.

36   Pease, "The sin of silence: The epidemic of denial about sexual abuse in the evangelical church".

37   Dr. Richard J. Krejcir, "Statistics on Pastors," *Into Thy Word— Teaching People How to Study the Bible*, accessed January 18, 2019, http://www.intothyword.org/apps/articles/?articleid=36562.

38   Rob Baker and Maria Dal Maso, *Clergy Sexual Misconduct: A Systems Approach to Prevention, Intervention, and Oversight*, ed. John Thoburn, (Carefree, Arizona: Gentle Path Press, 2011).

39   Ibid.

40   Marshall Segal, "When Leaders Fall, All Are Punished," *Desiring God*, last modified June 24, 2015, https://www.desiringgod.org/articles/when-leaders-fall-all-are-punished.

41   Paul Tautges, "12 Ways Satan May Try to Destroy You, Pastor," *Crosswalk.com*, last modified June 26, 2017, https://www.crosswalk.com/church/pastors-or-leadership/12-ways-satan-may-try-to-destroy-you-pastor.html.

42   Joel R. Beeke and Mark Jones, *A Puritan Theology: Doctrine for Life*, (Grand Rapids, Michigan: Reformation Heritage Books, 2012).

43   *NIV Life in the Spirit Study Bible*, (Grand Rapids, Michigan: Zondervan Publishing Company, 2003), 1914.

Chapter 5: Learning from David

44   Margaret Singleton and Ray Stephens, "My True Confession," last modified 1961, https://www.lyrics.com/lyric/26792273/Version+Galore/True+Confession.

45   Ray Pritchard, "Commentary on Ps. 51", modified March 2017, www.keepbelieving.com/scriptures/Psalms-51.

46   Andy Stanley, *Enemies of the Heart, Breaking Free from the Four Emotions that Control You* (Colorado: Multnomah Press, 2014), 203.

47   David Guzik, "Psalm 51 Bible Commentary," https://biblehub.com/commentaries/guzik/psalms/51.htm.

48   J. Oswald Sanders, *Enjoying Intimacy with God*, (Grand Rapids, Michigan: Discovery House Publishers, 2000), 53.

49   Ibid, 54.

50   Adam Clarke, "Psalm 51 Adam Clarke's Commentary", https://www.studylight.org/commentaries/acc/psalms-51.html.

51   Ray Steadman, "Psalm 51 by Ray Steadman", modified 1969, www.raysteadman.org.

52   Ibid.

53   Ibid.

54   David Guzik, "Psalm 51—Restoration of a Broken and Contrite King", https://enduringword.com.

55   Sanders, 54.

56   Guzik, Ps. 51.

57   Ibid.

58   Rosaria Champagne Butterfield, *Openness Unhindered,* 55.

59   Pritchard, Ps. 51.

60   John Piper, "Messages on Psalm 51 | Desiring God", https://www.desiringgod.org/scripture/psalms/51/messages.

61   Guzik, Ps. 51.

62   Ibid.

63   Ibid.

64   Sanders.

65   Steadman.

66   Guzik.

67   Steadman.

68   Pritchard.

69 Ibid.
70 Steadman.
71 Clarke.
72 Piper.
73 NLT Study Bible, 949, Verse 11.
74 Pritchard.
75 Adam Clarke's Commentary.
76 Ibid.
77 Ibid.
78 Piper.
79 Watchman Nee, *The Normal Christian Life,* (Kingsway Publication Eastbourne, 1982), 179.
80 NLT Study Bible, 949, verses 18-19.
81 Steadman, Ibid.
82 J. Oswald Sanders, 53.
83 J.D. Mallory, *"Mooing Cows and Bleating Sheep",* A sermon preached on February 19, 2017 at Stone Church, Toronto, ON. www.stonechurch.ca.

Chapter 6: Renewed by His Love

84 *NLT Study Bible,* Luke 15:11-32.
85 Keller, Timothy, *The Prodigal God, Recovering the Heart of the Christian Faith,* (New York: Penguin Books, 2008).
86 Ibid, xiv, xv.
87 Keller, 17-28. In these two chapters, Keller shows that both brothers sinned against their father and failed to serve him for the right reason.
88 Cory Asbury, Caleb Culver, and Ran Jackson, "Reckless Love" (California: Bethel Music Publishing (ASCAP) / Watershed Publishing Group (ASCAP), 2017).
89 Asbury, https://relevantmagazine.com/god/cory-asbury-reckless-love-the-sunday-staple-sweeping-the-nation-exerts-honesty-and-power/.
90 Asbury, https://godtv.com/ the-story-behind-cory-asburys-powerful-song-reckless-love/.

91 Phil Wickham, "This is Amazing Grace: The Story Behind the Song", posted Sept. 24, 2013 by www.newreleasetoday.com, https://www.newreleasetoday.com/article.php?article_id=1184.

92 Josh Farro, Phil Wickham, Jeremy Riddle, "This is Amazing Grace", © 2012 Warner/Chappell Music, Inc. (ASCAP)/Seems Like Music (BMI)/Phil Wickham Music (BMI) (admin by Simpleville Publishing, LLC) /Bethel Music Publishing (ASCAP).

Chapter 7: Discovering Me

93 Milan and Kay Yerkovich, *How We Love: Discover Your Love Style, Enhance Your Marriage,* (New York: Water Brook Press, 2016), 31.

94 Ibid, 32.

95 A brief biography of Theophrastus, https://www.britanica.com/biography/Theophrastus.

96 Mark Grant, *Galen on Food and Diet* (London and New York: Routledge, 2000), https://en.wikipedia.org/wiki/Galen.

97 Joseph Chris, "The Melancholy Personality Type", Houston, TX, 2016, prepareforpsychologicaltest.com/melancholy-personality-type/.

98 Ibid.

99 Mervin Byrd, "Transforming Minds", Personality Trait, Personality Type-Melancholic https://www.youtube.com/playlist?list=PL72181A1 4FC7DF812.

100 Byrd, prepareforpsychologicaltest.com/choleric-personality-type/.

101 Ibid, Choleric.

102 Aurum, "The Four Temperaments", 2014. http://fourtemperaments.com/4-primary-temperaments/).

103 Byrd, Sanguine.

104 Ibid.

105 Byrd, Phlegmatic.

106 Ibid.

107 Dr. Tom Knots, "The Four Temperaments Video, the Phlegmatic Personality", May 5, 2017, https://www.youtube.com/watch?v=CankeStpLIU.

108 Tobias Cornwall, "The Four Temperaments", http://temperaments.fighunter.com/?page=test.

109 Dr. Bing, "The Four Temperaments Test",
    https://psychologia.co/four-temperaments-test/.
110 Milan and Kay Yerkovich, *How We Love.* The Love Style Quiz,
    https://howwelove.com/love-style-quiz/love-style-quiz-results.
111 Milan and Kay Yerkovich, 50.
112 Gary L. McIntosh and Samuel D. Rima, *"Overcoming...", 106.*
113 Ibid, 107.
114 Ibid, 115.
115 Ibid, 116.
116 Ibid, 122-123.
117 Ibid, 123.
118 Ibid, 135.
119 Ibid, 143.
120 Ibid, 140-141.
121 Ibid, 141.
122 C. Gene Wilkes, *Jesus on Leadership, Discovering the Secrets of
    Servant Leadership from the Life of Christ*, (Wheaton, IL: Tyndale
    House Publishers, 1998), 25.
123 Gary L. McIntosh and Samuel D. Rima, *"Overcoming..."*, 133.
124 Ibid, 136.
125 John Thoburn and Rob Baker with Maria Dal Maso, C*lergy Sexual
    Misconduct: A Systems Approach to Prevention,* (AZ: Gentle Path
    Press, 2011).
126 Garrett Kell, *The Pattern Among Fallen Pastors*,
    http://gracefall.org/pastors-secrets/the-statistics/.
127 Ibid.
128 Ibid.
129 Nietzsche, F.W. & Kaufman, W.A. *The Portable Nietzsche*, (New York:
    Penguin Classics, 1982).

Chapter 8: Renovating the Heart

130 Dr. Harry W. Schaumburg, *False Intimacy, Understanding the
    Struggle of Sexual Addiction,* (Colorado Springs, CO: NavPress,
    Tyndale House Publishers, Inc., 1997), 140.
131 Willard, *Renovation of the Heart.*
132 Ibid, 14.

133 Test administered: Minnesota Multiphasic Inventory (MMPI-2), the Personal Problems Checklist for Adults, Sentence Completion Blank Adult Form, and the Millon Clinical Multiaxial Inventory-III (MCMI-III).

134 Willard, *Renovation of the Heart*, 96.

135 Ibid, 98.

136 Ibid, 112.

137 Timothy Keller, *The Reason for God, Belief in an Age of Skepticism*, (New York, NY: Riverhead Books, 2008), 168.

138 Philip Yancey, *What's So Amazing About Grace* (Grand Rapids, Michigan: Zondervan Publishing House, 1997), 201.

139 Barbara B. Taylor, *Speaking of Sin: The Lost Language of Salvation*, (Cowley Publications, 2000), 57-67.

140 NIV Study Bible Commentary, 1034.

Chapter 9: Restoration

* Some content in this chapter has been taken from RENOVATION OF THE HEART, by Dallas Willard. Copyright 2002. Used by permission of NavPress. All rights reserved. Represented by Tyndale House Publishers, Inc.

141 Funk and Wagnalls, Canadian College Dictionary (Markham, ON: Harper and Row Publishers, Inc., 1986), 1147.

142 Earl & Sandy Wilson, Paul & Virginia Friesen, and Larry & Nancy Paulson, *Restoring the Fallen: A Team Approach to Caring, Confronting & Reconciling* (Downers Grove, IL: InterVarsity Press, 1997).

143 Ibid, 11.

144 Eric Geiger, "3 Views of Restoring a Fallen Pastor," last modified July 18, 2016.
    https://ericgeiger.com/2016/07/3-different-views-of-restoration/.

145 *Hymns of Glorious Praise* (Springfield, Missouri: Gospel Publishing House, 1969), 200.

ABOUT THE AUTHOR

COLIN GITTENS WAS born in Guyana, South America, and came to Canada in 1972. Originally a school teacher, Colin felt a clear call from God to prepare for full-time ministry in 1984. After graduating from Eastern Pentecostal Bible College (now Masters' College and Seminary) in 1987, he received his pastoral credentials from the Pentecostal Assemblies of Canada (PAOC).

For over three decades, Colin has pastored three congregations and ministered in various prisons. After resigning from his church, he intentionally followed a restoration program, sought counselling, and relied on the Holy Spirit to restore his heart to the place where he once enjoyed intimacy with God.

He wrote Pursued by Grace because if his fall and removal from ministry can serve to help even one other leader from succumbing to temptation, then telling his story would be worth it all. He remains forever thankful that "God sent His loving grace to pursue me, stop me in my tracks, turn me around, and bring me back into His fold."

Today, Colin and his wife Dorselie attend a PAOC church and reside in the Greater Toronto area. They have three children and four grandchildren.

FOR MORE INFORMATION VISIT:
WWW.PURSUEDBYGRACE.ORG